WHAT A
GRL
NEEDS
FROM HER
M M

Books by Cheri Fuller

FROM BETHANY HOUSE PUBLISHERS

What a Girl Needs From Her Mom
What a Son Needs From His Mom

WHAT A
G*RL
NEEDS
FROM HER
M*M

CHERI FULLER

BETHANY HOUSE PUBLISHERS
a division of Baker Publishing Group
Minneapolis, Minnesota

Published by Bethany House Publishers
11400 Hampshire Avenue South
Bloomington, Minnesota 55438
www.bethanyhouse.com

Bethany House Publishers is a division of
Baker Publishing Group, Grand Rapids, Michigan

Printed in the United States of America

Library of Congress Cataloging-in-Publication Data

Fuller, Cheri.
    What a girl needs from her mom / Cheri Fuller.
        pages cm
    Includes bibliographical references.
    Summary: "Presents advice to moms on how to better understand their daughters' needs, provide guidance to girls of different ages, encourage femininity and spiritual growth, and raise them as healthy, confident young women"— Provided by publisher.
    ISBN 978-0-7642-1224-6 (pbk. : alk. paper)
    1. Mothers and daughters. 2. Daughters—Psychology. 3. Child rearing. 4. Mothers and daughters—Religious aspects—Christianity. I. Title.
HQ755.85.F852 2015
306.874′3—dc23   2014041507

Cover design by LOOK Design Studio

Author is represented by WordServe Literary Agency

15   16   17   18   19   20   21   7   6   5   4   3   2   1

In keeping with biblical principles of creation stewardship, Baker Publishing Group advocates the responsible use of our natural resources. As a member of the Green Press Initiative, our company uses recycled paper when possible. The text paper of this book is composed in part of post-consumer waste.

To
Alison Delaine Fuller Plum,
my creative, talented,
courageous daughter.

Love you forever
and like you for always.
As long as I'm living
your mama I'll be.*

*Adapted from one of my favorite children's books,
Love You Forever by Robert Munsch.

Contents

Contents

1

Mothering in a Changing World

A mother's treasure is her daughter.

Catherine Pulsifer

When Erin first saw her baby girl on the ultrasound, her heart beat a staccato rhythm and she gasped in delight. A daughter! *Compared to raising our boy, this will be a breeze,* she thought. After all, Erin had been a young girl once and understood the stages her daughter would navigate. And it *was* smooth sailing for the first two years; Erin had fun putting cute pink outfits and matching headbands and bows on Emma and posting photos on Instagram. But after Erin saw her Emma walking around with one hand on her little hip and the other holding Mom's cell phone to her ear talking up a storm, it took her aback. When Erin's high-spirited, strong-willed daughter overpowered her big brother and barked orders, she thought, *Uh-oh. Maybe this isn't going to be the cakewalk I thought it would be.*

A few years later, Erin was picking Emma up at school one afternoon and observed a line of eight kindergarten boys leaning against the building, waiting for their rides while on their iPads. Erin could only shake her head about how quickly the world was changing.

Later she was baffled by questions Emma asked when only in the third grade: "Mommy, what is an STD?" and "Why does Jenny have two mommies?"

The older Emma gets, the more mystified her mom feels about the situations she and her peers are facing.

Erin is not alone in her puzzlement. Our girls are growing up in a different generation and culture than we did. Kathryn, a mother of three, told me she wasn't prepared for her normal-weight ten-year-old daughter to come home in tears and say she was fat and disgusting. "Who gave you that idea?" Kathryn asked.

"The girls on the playground said I was. And they sent me a mean message on Instagram."

Kathryn had no idea what a big part social media played in her daughter's school or how obsessed girls were with being thin.

"There were movie stars when I was growing up," Kathryn said, "but now these highly sexualized, super-skinny images of girls and women whose bodies and faces have been airbrushed to perfection are everywhere, constantly barraging our girls with false expectations of how they're supposed to look."

"Social media definitely wasn't around when I was growing up," said Maggie, a Texas mom. "All the ins and outs of this very voyeuristic and affirmation-seeking culture mean I've needed to have more conversations about where my daughters find their worth.

"I never knew I'd be discussing what they shouldn't put on the Internet, in terms of appropriateness or the way they're portraying themselves, because it's out there forever. They're only twelve and eight!"

Maybe you have had similar thoughts as Erin did: *I was a girl once; I'll know what's going on with my daughter.* But at a certain point you realized that your daughter is growing up in an entirely different world that's technology-driven and changing rapidly. A world in which children are exposed to a wider range of experiences than we ever imagined. A world that's blurring the lines between adult and child, exposing children to situations that aren't appropriate for their development level and to digital content that promotes self-harm, pornography, suicide, and even intense violence.

Many moms I've interviewed find it distressing that they not only need to be present and involved with their children's *physical life* (caring for them and keeping them safe and healthy in real time), but they need to be engaged in their girls' *Internet world*. Moms are already crazy-busy just getting the daily tasks of parenting done. The digital revolution has produced a whole new need that girls have: for their moms to help them navigate the digital world.

And our daughters need our help in other, not-so-apparent ways too.

The Adventure of Raising a Girl

There was something familiar and natural about giving birth to a girl, but I soon discovered how different Alison and I were. And though I was pretty sure I'd understand what it would be like for her to go through situations I'd faced, like puberty, for example, what I found is that Alison approached each stage with a unique perspective and temperament that was often a polar opposite to mine.

Alison's late teen years and early twenties were rocky as we sought to reconcile differences and accept each other fully, but today we are dear friends.

Yes, raising a girl is a rewarding, sometimes puzzling journey full of challenges and joys, surprises and obstacles. There can be months or years of smooth sailing and then seasons of turbulent times with our girls.

My British friend Debb Hackett is the mother of two young daughters, Grace and Olivia. Debb sent me a picture of their family careening down a giant slide, and shared, "Much like the photo, raising daughters is an adventure. Some days it's just lovely with Grace and Ollie playing dolls, doing hair, fashion shows, and cuddles. Other days they are out of sorts, fighting and in tears instead of getting along. It's hard when I hear or see stories of young girls who've been hurt. I struggle not to project that forward onto my girls; then parenting becomes all about trying to raise girls who avoid bad things rather than raising strong and responsible, loving young women."

Debb recounted the joys she has experienced in raising her girls from the moment each was born. "I was thrilled both times. We just wanted healthy babies. I felt and still feel very protective of them—their bodies, hearts, and minds. But mostly, I was simply overwhelmed by love."

She's grateful for a small hand in hers, skipping, blowing bubbles, building snow forts, sharing iced cookies, hearing "Mummy," and the great privilege of being the one whom her little girls run to whenever they are in tears.

Growing Up in a Girl World

I can identify with Debb's elation. My daughter, Alison, grew tired of hearing how absolutely thrilled we were when she was born. But it's true. After having two boys whom I loved dearly, my first and only daughter was a welcome, much-awaited surprise.

I come from a family of five girls—I'm the middle one—so I grew up in a girls' world, each of us jockeying for attention. I knew girl stuff: ruffled dresses Mama sewed for us, the dolls we got on Christmas, playing jacks on the kitchen floor and red rover outside, dressing up and giggling long after lights were out. Brother George was the number-six Heath child, the long-awaited prince. His Davy Crockett, stick horse, and tricycle world was a far stretch from our girly world. And he didn't have to vie for attention; he was the *only boy*.

Even from a young age I loved makeup and put it on whenever I could sneak some from my older sisters. I watched them roll their hair up at night and brush out their beautiful thick, dark waves in the morning. So when I was six years old, I got Mama to buy me some little pink foam rollers. That night I began a routine I continued for years: rolling my fine, straight hair so it would look curly in the morning, even though it never lasted past lunch.

Growing Pains

Fast-forward many years to the day I was rolling my three-year-old's blond hair in pink foam rollers. (No, not my old rollers; they'd long since fallen apart from use). Ali had seen them in a store and just had to have them. She thought it was great fun to have her whole head in pink rollers.

Yet only a few years later, when she was six, I was braiding her hair when she announced, "Mom, I learned how to French braid. I'll do it myself from now on." My heart sank a bit recalling the little girl who had let me put bows in her ponytails and create cute updos.

The closer Ali got to puberty, the more moody my previously sweet little girl became. One day, when she was fifteen, I found her standing in the middle of her room, surrounded by piles of T-shirts, shorts, still-dirty laundry, and toiletries we'd just purchased for camp.

"Don't you think you'd better take a rain poncho since you'll be sleeping in a tent and camping out? What about tucking the stuff we just bought into your suitcase?" I asked, feeling a bit time-pressured since the bus was leaving in only forty minutes and she wasn't packed yet.

"I don't need your help packing, and I'm not taking any of that stuff, especially the poncho!" Ali answered, irritated at my interference. Within a few moments, our conversation escalated into anger. An uncomfortable silence accompanied us as I drove her to catch the bus for camp.

Where did my little girl go, the one who loved to be with me and ride bikes around the neighborhood and go to the park together and chat? I wondered on the way home, my heart heavy. *And what happened to that good relationship we used to have?* Snapshots of snuggling under a big quilt while reading to Ali at bedtime and after-school conversations we'd shared over hot cocoa drifted across my memory. Maybe that's why the tensions of adolescence came as such a big surprise to me. Suddenly, my suggestions on homework—or just about anything—were met by an argument or a big sigh of "Oh, Mom!"

When her room looked like nuclear fallout, she resented my reminders to clean it. All I had to do was say "Mom things," as she called my comments, and she found me irritating.

Yes, the mother-daughter relationship can be intense, loving, and even strained at times. But oh, how we love our girls! Even when their entry into the world is a rough start.

Sugar and Spice and Everything Nice?

"Blissful" is not how many moms would describe their first days with their little sweethearts. Maybe the birth was traumatic because their baby was whisked off to the NICU for critical care. Or they were caught off guard by sad emotions and felt guilty for not being happier. Some talk about being overwhelmed by feelings of inadequacy.

"I know you think I'm going to say it was the deepest, most satisfying love, but honestly, after twenty-three hours of labor, I was beat!" my friend Stephanie told me, describing the day her daughter was born. "I was totally exhausted and overwhelmed."

When the nurse asked if Stephanie wanted to hold her baby in the moments after she was born, the new mom said, "No!" Baby Micah was a tiny, fragile-looking thing—a "cream-covered blob," Stephanie said. Micah was barely six pounds and had come three and a half weeks early. Stephanie called her mother from the hospital, crying, because she hadn't finished painting the baby's closet and didn't feel ready for her to arrive.

Grandma took care of that detail, and day-by-day, Stephanie fell more and more in love with her daughter. She was pure joy as she grew. No terrible twos. No toddler tantrums. "I honestly remember writing on her pre-K application that Micah had never been cross or had a bad day," Stephanie said.

The tween years—that's another story! *Challenging* is how Stephanie describes her daughter's current phase, mostly because she's entered the "pulling away" phase.

The Power of a Mom's Love

Yet no matter the challenges, whether we are younger or older moms, single moms or married with a supportive husband—there is nothing as powerful as the love of a mom for her daughter.

Our girls are gifts from God. But getting from that memorable day when we welcome them into our lives, through the infant and toddler years, and then the elementary and middle school years and beyond—all the growing pains, baffling times, school days, sick days, adolescent angst and drama . . . to the point somewhere down the road when our girls are grown up and we become adult friends—what an adventure it is!

All along the way, mothering takes patience and grace, tremendous strength and humility, a heart full of love and faith, and the warmth and security that helps girls thrive. Most of all, it takes a real understanding of our daughter's needs.

My mother had five daughters, and none of them were just alike. Girls don't all respond the same way. Each has a different emotional style, different temperament traits and gifts, unique ways of processing information and perceiving their experiences and the world around them. Some girls mature earlier, and others tend to be late developers in the physical, mental, or emotional areas. Some are intense in regard to emotions and relationships, and other girls are more mellow. That's why it's important to aim at understanding your daughter and what her needs are at different ages, as we will do in the pages ahead.

That's what this book is all about—unpacking what a girl needs from her mom. From connecting with your little girl in the early years to staying connected in the preteen and adolescent years, building her confidence and supporting her unique femininity. We'll also look at the needs girls have as they grow: the need for an emotional supporter, a mom who helps develop her potential and encourages her to dream big, a mom who fosters her daughter's learning, a mom who is present and engaged rather than distracted, who helps her precious girl navigate the digital world, who is intentional about taking time for communication and character-building, and a mother who nurtures her daughter's faith.

We will also look at some vital things that a mother provides, such as a listening ear so your daughter knows she can open up and talk about anything, through the transitions from middle school to high school to her launch into college and beyond. And a mom who can help her deal with societal pressures and messages about body image that she will be exposed to on TV and the Internet, at school or at sleepovers.

Most of all, we'll consider the greatest need in our girls' lives, which is our most powerful influence: being a mom who prays for her daughter faithfully and perseveringly throughout her life and never gives up.

No Perfect Moms

I want you to know that I don't approach the subject of raising children as if there is some magic formula or that we can do parenting in a "just perfect" way. Or in the perspective of "Do this and this, and your daughter will turn out this way." We do our part, we trust God to do His part, but our daughter has a will and makes choices about who she becomes.

The truth is, the perfect mother = perfect child concept is a myth, so I won't be promoting it. If we aim for perfection and expect the result of our earnest efforts or parenting formula to be an ideal young woman who pleases us and goes in just the direction we've planned, with no bumps in the road, then we may likely be very disappointed—not only in ourselves, but in our daughters and in God.

There is no perfect family, mom, dad, daughter, or son. The good news, though, is that although God doesn't promise an easy ride, He does promise to *always* be with us in the humbling, sometimes messy, marvelous privilege and responsibility of being our daughter's mother. I've found over and over that you can depend on the Lord's never-ending and always available grace to nurture and love your daughter, whatever age she is now and in the future, whether adopted or your biological daughter—because you were chosen of all the women in the world to be her mother.

Instead of simple recipes or formulas for raising the perfect girl, this book offers my experiences—including mistakes—and stories of other mothers. It also includes insights intended to help you understand your girl's needs better. Understanding and awareness are the first steps to meeting her needs, to building a loving, trusting relationship, and to staying connected throughout her life, even when she grows up and moves away.

You'll notice that the content of this book spans different ages and has helpful ideas for various stages, whether your daughter is four or seventeen. There's a lot in here for you!

You'll also find a section called "Questions to Discuss or Journal" that accompanies each chapter so you can use this book as a resource for your moms' group or small group. The questions can stimulate a lively group discussion, whether you do that via email with a few girlfriends across the world or in person, or right in your community or church.

I know you love your daughter very much or you wouldn't have bought this book, and I pray blessings on you as you read the pages ahead. Thanks for coming along on the journey of discovering what a girl needs from her mom.

2

A Mom Who Bonds and Connects With Her Daughter

> There is no more sacred undertaking than the care,
> support, and nurturing of a new life, and there is
> little we can ever do in our lives that will approach the
> awesome impact that our children have on our lives.
>
> Will Glennon

There are books full of information on mother-child attachment; there's no shortage of ways to bond with your little girl—*even before she is born*! One common recommendation is to get comfy on the sofa and read your favorite book to your baby bump.[1] From about twenty weeks in the womb, babies can hear their mother's heartbeat and recognize voices, especially Mom's voice. So talking to her is always a recommended activity.

And from twenty weeks, babies can distinguish between Mom's or Dad's touch and that of a stranger—aren't infants so smart? So giving your bump a gentle massage with lavender oil is said to help bonding. While you are expecting, singing is also highly recommended. And without your knowing it, all during the time you're carrying your little one, she is building a biochemical bond with you even before she makes her appearance on planet earth. And that mother-baby connection continues when you're holding your infant in the early days and weeks of life—even in the way you look into your baby's eyes.

This week I was presenting a teaching training seminar at a preschool, and one of the teachers told me she had recently attended a fascinating seminar. There she learned that neuroscientists have hooked electrodes up to the brain to see what parts of the brain light up when different emotions are experienced. The researchers were surprised to discover that the strongest emotion measured is in the infant brain when mother and baby first look at each other. The baby's eyes connect with her mom, and boom—the mother-infant gaze happens. That's also when the baby begins to recognize the voice and smell of her mother.

This is one reason why breastfeeding is so important. Whether breastfeeding or bottle feeding, most of the time the baby is looking right into her mother's eyes. These are significant moments of bonding.

Studies show surges of brain activity—literally the brain lighting up in certain key areas—occur when the baby experiences self-worth, safety, confidence—all essential to emotional development.

Do you remember the first time your baby girl smiled and you smiled back? Babies learn a great deal from how responsive parents are to them; it doesn't take them long to catch on to the fact that their actions—smiles, tears, excitement—get a predictable response (*every time I smile, Mommy smiles back*, she learns). Babies like to be imitated, scientists say. When we exaggerate their behavior or expressions back to them, it helps them understand themselves and how they're feeling. Isn't it amazing how truly smart babies are?

Love You Forever

One day when I was visiting our son and daughter-in-law in Wisconsin, Maggie was changing seven-month-old Lucy's diaper. Our little redheaded granddaughter's face lit up when her mom playfully slid a thin diaper across her face and asked in an animated voice, "Where is Lucy? Peekaboo, I see you!"

Lucy giggled and kicked her little feet, waving her arms up and down. "Mama, dada, ooooh!" Lucy squealed as her face lit up with a big smile.

"Daddy will be home in a little while, Lucy. He's at the hospital working," Maggie said. "Let's get your jammies on and read until he gets here."

As Maggie finished dressing Lucy, Josephine, her big sister, came into the room and waved a Beanie Babies rabbit before giving it to Lucy. Then Maggie scooped Lucy up into the comfy rocking chair and put her arm around Jos as she began to read the book *Love You Forever* to the girls.

Maggie's gentle physical touch, her cuddling, feeding, hugging, peekaboo games, and smiles played an important part in Lucy's brain development and growth, but they also powerfully connected them as mom and daughter. *Attachment* or bonding—that feeling of emotional connection between baby and mother—is a vital need in the first year or two of life. And those simple, caring expressions of love are all part of nurturing your little girl.

Attachment also includes soothing babies when they're fussy, including speaking in "motherese" or singing to them. Dr. Brenda Hunter, psychologist and author of *The Power of Mother Love*, says that when moms speak in their motherese voices, it's far more stimulating to them than a "cell phone" voice. And does she ever love to hear you sing, even if you don't think you have a good voice. After all, she heard your voice as you carried her for nine months, so your voice is the most comforting and familiar.

Researchers have reported that skin-to-skin contact between baby and mother can be a benefit to both. In addition, they are discovering that "consistent emotional engagement with infants can speed their development and recognition of self. Particularly in the newborn period, it helps calm babies: they cry less and it helps them sleep better. There are some studies that show their brain development is boosted—probably because they are calmer and sleep better, and in the first three months enabled the babies to be more responsive as well."[2]

Skin-to-skin contact in the first three months also seems to help mothers (and fathers) reduce their stress levels, decrease depression, and enable them to be more responsive to their babies' cues and needs and to be more connected.[3]

Smiling and singing, rocking your baby girl, and taking her out in the stroller, or reassuring her when she wakes up crying in the night—all these behaviors build the bond and connection that contribute to her feelings of being loved, belonging, and having a sense of safety—factors that nurture emotional security.

"It all starts in the first year of life," Dr. Hunter says. "If you have a close emotional bond with your baby girl and if you get it right early on, the whole of life is so much better for everybody."

Although you may be seriously tired and frazzled, six to twelve months of age is a significant time for your child. That's when your baby is "programmed or hardwired to fall in love with her mother, not her nanny or a string of caregivers," Dr. Hunter explains. "The infant falls in love with Mom first and then Dad during those important months. That's why if mothers have to go back to work, the worst time to do that is between six and twelve months.

"And if she does have to go back to work," Dr. Hunter advises, "Grandma, Daddy, or a very loving, *consistent* caregiver is far better for the child. You get a qualitatively different kind of child in the first two years who is cared for by a loving, affectionate mother/dad/grandma or a nurturing, responsive and loving consistent person versus a child that goes to group or day care. Day-care workers are notoriously transient so day care is a last resort." For many years, Dr. Hunter has been a champion and advocate of babies, addressed national conventions and congressional staff on childcare issues, and worked with two presidential commissions.

Dr. Hunter believes, and research shows, that if you want to be emotionally close with your teenage daughter, *be there the first year of life and form a loving, secure emotional bond with her.*

Every girl, little or big, needs a mom who's crazy about her— who will put her welfare before career ambitions, the acquisition of things, even a new love relationship—a mommy who loves her unconditionally and who can form a strong relationship with her that lasts a lifetime.

When Bonding Is Interrupted

Sometimes there are interruptions in attachment caused by trauma, medical complications, postpartum depression, mental illness, or PTSD (post-traumatic stress disorder). These conditions can interfere with the mother's ability to bond and sensitively respond to the infant's needs, but they aren't insurmountable.

One type of treatment, parent-child interaction therapy, is geared toward helping babies and young children and their parents reattach and bond. It is very directive, and the therapist coaches the mother and father on how to be more attuned to their children.

When parents are attuned to their child's needs, it teaches the child the importance of healthy, trusting, intimate relationships, but it also teaches the child *her own value* and the importance of eventually recognizing and taking care of her own needs.[4]

Bonding Is a Process: New Moms' Feelings

Because bonding is so important, we put pressure on ourselves and expect it to happen at a particular time and in a way our girlfriend or mom said she experienced it. But that's not always the case. Katie, a young mother I know, loved the pregnancy part, but when Caroline was born, her mind was flooded with future concerns like, *Oh my, junior high's coming; girls are so mean to each other.*

Katie and her friend Shauna and their little girls were having coffee with me at Panera one day when Katie described her experience of being a first-time mom. "I'd been healthy and was excited to be a mom, so the sad feelings after my first baby arrived surprised me. I heard people saying, 'This is the best time of your life,' and I felt worthless because it was *not* the best time for me."

"I felt like that too," Shauna added. "Why didn't anybody tell me? At first I just wanted to run away. The delivery was wonderful, but when we went home, I had no emotion. I was detached; there was nothing. I was just sad for a while."

Katie described how she felt: "I had postpartum depression too but didn't know it yet. I was teary and sad the whole week we were in the hospital. I was actually scared of my baby. Caroline had jaundice, and it was a bad delivery. She was bruised. The nurses had her under the lights and they were pumping her with fluids. When I saw her lying there, it was absolutely terrifying. I was in despair. When I talked to my doctor, I couldn't stop crying."

After they got home, whenever Katie got in the car to go to the grocery store by herself, her mom and husband would ask, "Are you coming back?" She had a friend dealing with infertility, so Katie thought, *Problem solved: If I give them our baby, everything will go back to normal.*

She knew those thoughts were crazy and never mentioned it to her husband. But even after a few weeks, she still didn't want to touch her baby. "I just thought it would be better if I weren't here and wasn't her mother."

The only thing that went well was breastfeeding. During this time, Katie became pregnant with their son and her husband lost his job. "It was a firehose of awfulness," she said. "In Dallas, our church didn't understand, and was unkind and spiritually abusive. We had no insurance. We didn't know if family support would be there. We had paid cash for Caroline's delivery and worried about how we'd pay for the second baby's delivery."

Yet as both Katie and Shauna's girls have grown, their joys have multiplied: On Shauna's girls' nights with Bree (five) and Ally (three), their favorite thing is to go get red mango ice cream. The girls get to pick the toppings. They paint fingernails and toenails and have such fun. Caroline, Katie's daughter, is five and loves to talk with her mom, shop with her, and pick out accessories. She's very affectionate, very sweet and cuddly to be with, especially one-on-one.[5]

Mothers have very high expectations for themselves; they expect they'll know what to do and how to feel about a new baby—and are terrified if they don't. "But for many of us, this is a brand-new experience. And there really isn't one way to do it right. Megan Aston, assistant professor of nursing at Dalhousie University in Halifax, says, 'It isn't realistic to expect to have that comfort zone immediately—it just happens in its own time. The relationship develops, the bonding continues.'"[6] Midwife Jaylene Mory says, "I look at bonding as a long-term process. It's not a one-time event. There are ongoing opportunities over the days after the birth, and the weeks, months and years to come, to create, enhance and deepen the connection with your baby."[7]

While there are countless studies on the importance of early bonding, there is also evidence that orphans and kids who didn't have a chance to bond with their parents early on can develop strong bonds with other people (like adoptive parents) and "sound emotional and social development." Although you'd love to bond with your baby in the first few hours, and it's advantageous to do so, "there are still plenty of opportunities down the road. . . . It matters not only what happens immediately after but in the months and years that come," said Daniel Lagace-Seguin, professor of psychology at Mount Saint Vincent, England.

Postpartum Depression

One thing many moms encounter in the early days after their baby is born is the "baby blues." Insomnia, sadness, mood swings, and some crying jags in the first few days following labor and delivery are not terribly unusual because of the big hormonal changes at delivery and just after. Neither is feeling inadequate or scared, especially if this is your first child.

But if your symptoms persist more than a few weeks or your depression gets worse to the point that you are withdrawing from people and activities, having trouble nurturing your baby, are very restless and irritable, or having memory problems, you may have postpartum depression. PPD can hinder your ability to care for your child and last for up to a year or more, so it's vital to get treatment and support.

As Dr. Hunter explains, "Mother needs to be there physically and *emotionally* for her child. If she's depressed, she's emotionally unavailable."[8] When Dr. Hunter talks to moms, she encourages them to be a CSR mother, which means consistent, sensitive, and responsive. If you're depressed, you're more likely to be hostile, unresponsive, or rejecting to your child. If you have postpartum depression, she advises seeing your physician and treating it with medication rather than denying it or expecting it will go away.

So let me encourage you to *seek help* if you experience this cluster of symptoms, because it will make a big difference in how you nurture your little girl and how much you enjoy your first year of her life.

And if you're too depressed to try to get an appointment for yourself or you have trouble speaking to the doctor about how you feel, have a girlfriend or mother come alongside so you don't quit until you get the help you need. There is no shame in getting treatment for postpartum depression—it's the wisest thing to do for you and your little girl.

Kids, Moms, and Technology

Since so many moms put an effort into bonding with their baby during the pregnancy and in the first months and year, it seems a shame to lose that connection due to the bombarding of technology around us.

We're a culture and generation addicted to lightning-fast technology and to constant communication via smartphones and digital devices. We're surrounded by noise and are exceedingly distracted—and this can negatively affect the connection between parent and child.

Child development experts are seeing an epidemic of loneliness, from young kids to high school students. Dr. Hunter recently interviewed a seventh-grade teacher who said that one-third of all the students in her classroom tested as gifted. There are more PhDs among the parents in this school than anywhere else in the U.S., yet the kids are starved for relationship. Most of the kids go home to an empty house. Instead of a mother to greet them, there is a twenty-dollar bill on the counter and a note that says, "Order a pizza for yourself." These highly educated parents have bright, very lonely kids.

"Moms need to be there throughout the child's years at home, after school and/or bedtime—not just physically present but emotionally present and engaged as well," Dr. Hunter says. "I urge the moms to spend at least ten minutes alone with each child every day. And be close to your daughter."

Her concern as a psychologist is this: "What makes us human? The ability to form a bond with God through Christ and a bond with people. If we cease to be connected, what are we then?"

As your daughter grows, at each state of development, prioritize enough time with her so she feels that you're a warm, affectionate mother. If you have that, you and your daughter can deal with almost anything; the storms that you may have to weather are much better weathered when you have a loving, trusting bond with your girls.[9]

Focused Attention

When my children were young, one of the most helpful concepts I learned was the importance of setting aside time for focused attention for each one. Although I did all the home responsibilities and often worked part time, we had lots of family time in the evening or during the day when I took the kids to the park, played guitar and sang kid songs together, or read books together.

But when I read Dr. Ross Campbell's *How to Really Love Your Child* and applied the practices of focused attention, I found our kids responded much better to teaching, training, and discipline.

Dr. Campbell later teamed up with Dr. Gary Chapman to write *The 5 Love Languages of Children* and shared more about what our children need. "Every child has an emotional tank, a place of emotional strength that can fuel him [or her] through the challenging days of childhood and adolescence," they wrote. "Just as cars are powered by reserves in the gas tank, our children are fueled from their emotional tanks. We must fill our children's emotional tanks for them to operate as they should and reach their potential. But with what do we fill these tanks? Love, of course . . ."[10]

What fills our children's emotional tanks is time spent with them, giving them focused attention (not distracted or interrupted by anything else), giving them eye contact, physical contact (like a pat on their arm or a hug), a listening ear, and doing something that they enjoy. In our family, we just called this "special time."

On a regular basis, for ten to twenty minutes, I did something with each child that they enjoyed. It wasn't every day, but I (or Holmes) would focus just on that child as we did an activity together. With our older sons, special time involved balls, Legos, board games, making Superman costumes, and later shooting hoops, playing tennis, and throwing the football or baseball, depending on the sports season and what the boys were into.

When Alison came along, coming up with ways to have special time with her was not a problem. As a toddler, she loved for me to get out a small tea set and little stuffed bears and have Muffy Bear tea parties. I dyed pre-made white icing pink with food coloring and we spread it on mini-marshmallows or little animal crackers for tea party treats arranged on the tiny plates. She poured tea (apple juice) into the little cups and we chatted over tea. The Muffy Bears and my daughter somehow seemed to eat all the treats up.

As she grew, Ali and I did active things like riding bikes, swinging at the park, and going on nature walks and collecting acorns, which we later painted faces on to make a family.

Actually, toddlers and preschoolers like to do whatever Mom is doing, from standing on a stepstool to "help" with dishes to stirring batter when you make a cake or whip up a batch of brownies. They just like hanging out with you. They even like having a toy broom and helping you sweep. Enjoy the help—it may not be so freely offered when they grow older.

Any creative ways of connecting, like making little Popsicle stick people while little brother is asleep, can be fun. Putting your daughter on your lap or right beside you while reading to her makes sweet connection times, not only at bedtime but also in the doctor's office when you're waiting. I always carried a few books with me for times when we had to wait, and used the time for reading or storytelling. Singing to our girls is always bonding. Lucinda, a Connecticut mom, always sang songs to her Maggie at bedtime from the time she was a baby through junior high. She sang old Frank Sinatra songs, love songs, and show tunes. She put Maggie's name in the song and sang about her love, just to encourage her and build a sense of security and love.

Arabella, a little blond-haired girl I met recently, pushed her sunglasses back on her bow headband as she told me, "I'm growing up. I'm four and my brother is two. We have two real bunnies that are hopping and jumping all around under our apple tree." After a few minutes of chatting with me, she added, "I went to Disney World and wore the mermaid dress, and Mommy pulled my hair back in a beautiful bun."

I found out all kinds of information as we sat together in the allergy doctor's waiting room: that her favorite place to go (after Disney World) is Inspirations in Edmond, Oklahoma, the city we live in. Her mom takes her there for a special high tea, just the two of them. She chatted about her baby brother and how she helps him, and what she's coloring. What a cutie Arabella is. She brightened up my day and everyone else's in the doctor's office.

My favorite place to see parents and children interacting is at the park, a place they can relax and laugh, run and sit, have a snack on a blanket on the grass, and just be together. Sadly, I see more and more parents pushing their kids on the swings while they talk on the phone or text. I hope you'll make time for many trips to the park or outings to feed ducks at a nearby pond sans tech device, trips to the zoo with your little girl to see and talk about all the funny and beautiful animals, times to lay on the grass and watch the stars together, and to lie beside her telling her a story when the lights are out.

As author Dorothy Evslin observed, "It will be gone before you know it. The fingerprints on the wall appear higher and higher. Then suddenly they disappear."

Connecting in the Midst of a Busy Career

Carol Hartzog, a media marketing consultant and editor, has a fulfilling career and two beautiful teenage daughters. We were having coffee one day when her girls were younger when she shared her frustration about not having enough time with them. Her daughters were only ten months apart, and there was lots of sister rivalry and desire for Mom's attention. Her husband worked long hours and had a plateful of responsibilities, especially in getting a new business up and going.

I encouraged Carol to be purposeful about having a week with each of her daughters in the summer doing what they'd most like to do. Carol took off with the idea and has added her own twists over the years. The first day of their special week, she and the daughter-of-the-week dive into cleaning and reorganizing the girl's bedroom. The next day they do some kind of volunteer service in the community together.

The next few days and nights, they go out of town on an adventure, just the two of them. The girls get to choose the music for the drive (Mom picked a few songs too). Elizabeth is her outdoor girl, so this summer she and Carol went to Beavers Bend State Park for a laid-back hiking and nature adventure. For a few years Hannah has picked shopping at the Galleria and staying in a hotel in Dallas. The girls are so close in age, Carol says to have total focus and unpressured time with each one alone has been so valuable to their relationship. And the girls love having their one week doing just want they want to do. It's is a real gift to them and to her.

Since she has her own business, Carol is able to arrange her schedule to take the time off with each girl. And it's been very worthwhile for all these summers for the memories they've made and the stronger connections they've built.

"I definitely love getting to have Mom one-on-one without my sister," Hannah told me. "Every year we've done this, Mom and I get closer." They make a memory box after each trip and stick in souvenirs and special things they found, and then each box goes at the top of their closets. The girls are now sixteen and fifteen and it won't be that long until they go to college, but they'll have very good memories to take along. They're also looking forward to more special weeks with their mom.

As they grow up, daughters still need their moms. In middle school, teachers often say that kids need their parents less. True, they are starting to become more independent, but do your best to stay connected in the middle school and high school years. They still need a real sense of belonging and connection with family.

Even when your daughter graduates from high school and she's taking flight and becoming her own person, she needs a healthy, loving connection with Mom.

There are lots of ways to do that. One idea is to walk (or run) for a cause. Choose a walkathon or 5K run like the Susan G. Komen Race for the Cure that you and your daughter can do together. Even if you live in different cities, participating in the same event but in different locations can be a shared experience.

Connection time might be a shopping expedition at vintage stores and flea markets, if that's your daughter's favorite. When you're together, get a manicure or pedicure, learn something new, or try a new restaurant. Read the same books (or audiobooks) and then talk about them on the phone.

There's no ideal formula for bonding, resolving conflicts, or reconnecting with your daughter, but my daughter and I discovered it can be healing and refreshing to just have fun together as mom and daughter. Dr. Ruth Nemzoff, who lectures widely on family dynamics, says, "One can communicate in many ways, and talking is only one of them. Sometimes we use words. Sometimes a bike ride or shopping trip serves to cement bonds or to recall happier times. . . . You can build a relationship on mutual interests, just as you would with a friend. Sharing experiences and bonding over

31

common hobbies is communicating. These intersections make great conversation starters."[11]

Questions to Discuss or Journal

1. I love what Dr. Hunter asks the many mothers she counsels. It is a profound question for each of us: Are your choices helping or hurting you? Are your choices helping or hurting your daughter?

2. What does your young girl need, or if she is older, what did you see as her greatest needs when she was in the first two or three years of life?

3. What was or is your favorite way of bonding and connecting with your baby? What frustrations did you have in the early months about attachment?

4. What is your daughter's favorite way to connect with you now?

5. What was most challenging in the early months or years of her life?

6. What are some of your most enjoyable ways of spending time with your daughter? Are they equally enjoyable for her?

3

A Mom Who Listens
With Her Heart

We could put ten-foot banners around the house
reminding our children how much we love them or
how special they are, and yet these will have far less
impact than a simple act of truly listening.

Steven Vannoy

I remember as a child *longing* for my mother to sit down and just talk with me and listen. But she was a very busy mom. With six children, she worked from dawn to past dusk keeping the house clean, preparing three meals a day, and washing all the laundry for eight people and usually many cloth diapers for the littlest one. She didn't go to bed until every item was washed and dried, folded, and put away. Add in washing all the dishes, pots, and pans after meals until the big girls could start helping, and just supervising six children—yikes, that's a lot of work!

She also made our clothes. Mama had a real sense of style and color, and loved to design our dresses, buy the fabric, and then spend hours sewing five frocks with added lace or piping. One year Mama made us five matching dresses for Easter. I couldn't wait until she finished and we got to wear them.

But that didn't leave a lot of time for Mama to sit down and talk with each one of us. Even so, after we'd walked home from school on many days, Mama would fix us cocoa or hot tea and cinnamon toast and ask how our school day had gone. Those were golden moments that I still remember, even though three or four of us may have been sharing her attention. I just wished there were more of those moments . . . and I still like cinnamon toast.

When I became a mother, I had the best of intentions to really listen to my children, but a multitude of tasks got in the way. There were all those casseroles to cook and laundry that needed to be done, and in some years a part-time teaching job with English papers to grade. And *then* I understood why my mom did not sit down every day to listen and talk with me.

Growing up with four sisters—all talkers—and then little brother George, who could barely get a word in edgewise, I became pretty good at talking. Listening? I had to work at that.

Your Best Influence: Listening

I'm not alone. Somewhere I read that women have so many words stored up to be said in a day, they are enough to fill sixty-six books in one year. Listening, especially with *our full attention*, is not what we do best. We're often too busy or too distracted or hurried.

Someone once said that the fact that God gave us two ears and one mouth should give us a clue about which to use the most. As James 1:19 says, "Everyone should be quick to listen, slow to speak and slow to become angry." An estimated 80 percent of the communication process is listening, yet it's often the most neglected and misunderstood.

Here's the real truth that struck me: Research shows that you have a greater impact on people by *how you listen* than *how you talk*.[1] However, if we're so busy or distracted on a regular basis that we don't listen when our girls are young, before long, we'll turn around a few times and their legs will be longer and shoe sizes past ours. Their schedules will be so hectic with sports, academics, friends, and activities that we'll have to make an appointment with them to spend time talking. And we'll wonder why our preteens and teens won't talk to us but wish with all our hearts that they would.

Roadblocks to Communication

As we've seen, the most important key to communication is listening to your daughter so she will talk and listen to you. Listen to her joys and heartaches, listen to her excitement and fears, hear her out when she's troubled or is discouraged by the inevitable disappointments, listen to the things she's stressed about regarding school or friends. Listen to her and you'll find that someday—maybe in the not-too-distant future—she'll come back to listen to you.

There are some major roadblocks that will hinder communication between us and our girls to consider avoiding:

- **Giving advice before hearing her out.** Counselors tell me that many moms can barely have a whole conversation with their children and teens without teaching, reminding, belittling, scolding, or cautioning.

- **Finishing her sentences.** Nothing shuts down a girl's communication faster than not being able to complete her own thoughts. Yikes, I used to do that until I discovered how absolutely annoying it is to both kids and adults. Many moms are guilty of this because we may think faster or think we know what our dear one is going to say. Be patient and encourage her to speak for herself.

- **Jumping in with positive thoughts to cheer her up when she's expressing sadness or anger** before hearing her out. This was one of my biggies. While conveying hope and encouragement is important, we may need to learn to restrain our positivity a bit and first listen to our daughter empathetically rather than trying to change her feelings. Otherwise, she may feel guilty about feeling bad or sad.

- **Tossing out orders or giving little lectures** when she walks in from school instead of asking how she's doing or how her day was.

- **Criticizing her.** Being critical of your daughter on an ongoing basis drives a wedge between the two of you—or sometimes a wall so big it's hard to scale.

Listening From the Heart

What a gift it is when a mom can give her daughter a listening ear and they can keep the lines of communication open. Dr. Thomas Lickona says, "The quality of our love often comes down to the quality of our communication."[2]

How are the communication lines between you and your daughter? I hear girls say over and over, especially those in middle school and high school, "What I need most from my mom is love and support, and especially someone to talk to, pour my heart out to, and tell everything to without being judged." When a girl knows her mom is there to listen and just be there for her without judging her, and to share advice when it's welcomed, it means the world to her.

Although I have had to work at being a better listener, my daughter, now a mom herself, says I have come a long way. Throughout her growing-up years, I learned some things I share below. Hopefully they will help you tune in to what your daughter is trying to say and to respond in a way that lets her know that when she wants to talk or discuss something, you'll be there to hear it. I call this listening from the heart.

Give eye contact and focused attention when your daughter is talking, and avoid gazing at your cell phone, iPad, or to-do list. Pay attention not just to her words, but also her expressions and body language.

Remember that some of the best times of communication occur at random, unexpected moments, especially late at night if you have teenage daughters, or at bedtime or after school for some girls. Still, if you're in the middle of a task you just must finish, ask her, "Can we set a time a little later today when we can talk about this?"

In addition to bedtime or late at night, some of the best opportunities come when you and your daughter are actively engaged in doing something she enjoys: whipping up a batch of cookies or ants on a log (celery sticks with peanut butter spread on them and dotted with raisins). Taking a walk together often spurs a little conversation. So does kicking a soccer ball. When she's heated up in physical activity, feelings and words often begin to flow.

Driving in the car can be an ideal place for connecting and communicating because you're both looking ahead and it's less intimidating. If you can take just one of your girls at a time it's even better. Wynne Terlizzi, a Chicago mom of three, calls her daughter Elona her "errand girl" because they have so much fun going to the grocery store together. Car outings are their favorite times to talk. It's amazing what kids will say when they're riding along with us in the car.

Let go of expectations. Sometimes when we would love to talk with our girls, they are just not in the mood. "It takes being attuned to where they are, and when moments open up, being quiet and listening," Tiffany (Tiff) Fuller said. Her two teenagers are good communicators (I know because they're my grandchildren), constantly growing and changing.

Tiff has tried to plan sharing times with Caitlin over a card game or lunch, and even had a few great conversation-starter questions to discuss, but sometimes those chats barely last a minute. "But there are times Caitlin brings something up and it becomes a forty-five-minute conversation. It's about being available," Tiff said.

Practice active listening. When your daughter tells you about being angry at her best friend for not inviting her to a sleepover, or when she's upset about not being chosen for a team at recess, hear her out—be an active listener. Don't rush in with comments like "You shouldn't feel like that." By not jumping in right away with your opinion, you give her time to fully express herself. It also helps you to be intentional about hearing the underlying message.

Then, before you ask a question or share your thoughts, you might want to summarize in a few words what you heard her say. This communicates respect and interest and encourages her to talk more, cry if she needs to, and simply know she's in a safe place. Reflecting her feelings back to her by saying, "It sounds like you're really hurt about being excluded like that," is so much more helpful than "I don't know why you're so angry and upset about this" or "It's not a big deal." Another good response is "Yes, I've had those kinds of feelings before," which lets her know she's not alone in experiencing anger or deep hurt.

Sometimes all it takes for a girl to feel better is to *feel heard and understood.* You don't have to solve or fix the whole problem.

Allow disagreement. When moms think they're always right and don't allow their daughters to disagree, it's a sign of over-control and will likely shut down conversation. The girl thinks, *Mom doesn't care about my opinion and won't let me share my views, so why try?* This is especially troubling when something big comes up that she *should* discuss with you.

Encourage questions. If questions are discouraged, a girl's independent thinking is squelched. Then there's no chance for discussion of different ideas, no chance for disagreement, and the potential for real conversation decreases dramatically. As a by-product, girls lose their desire to interact. It's much better to invite her into the conversation with questions such as, "What do you think of this issue?" or "How would you approach it?"

You don't have to agree with her opinions, but she'll feel respected when her ideas are welcomed and considered to have value. When there are decisions to be made, let her listen to your decision-making process and discuss the sides of an issue. Then ask how she sees it.

Focus on understanding her and her message rather than giving quick answers or telling her why she's wrong if you don't agree. Let her know you'll always be her ally and be on her side. If, for example, your daughter's friend Beth has been mean to your daughter, resist saying things like, "Just think how Beth feels; she probably is just lonely because her dad's on a business trip." Coming to a greater understanding of our girls lets us have a window of insight into how they're thinking, maybe why they act the way they do. That doesn't mean you don't correct her or you don't disagree with what she says and does—but that you're endeavoring to see where she's coming from.

Sometimes our daughters are so distressed by a circumstance that they don't want to talk about it right away. Let her know you'll be there when she's ready. You may *really* want to know what is troubling her, but try to be patient and trust that a good time to talk will come.

Avoid overreacting to sensitive subjects she may bring up. When we overreact, girls tend to clam up with us; instead, they talk about it with friends. Girls (especially during adolescence) don't tell their moms certain things when they expect disapproval. Likewise, they don't share problems when they anticipate it will make Mom become fearful or freak out. I know there were times I was so distressed with how sad my daughter sounded that I probably wasn't helpful at all. Oh, how we need God's grace and patience to be the listening ears our girls need.

It can be very difficult to be calm in the heat of a disagreement, but it's important. If you get emotionally upset and your voice is escalating by the minute, your daughter will likely not hear what you're saying. She may stay in the room if she has to, but she won't be emotionally present.

Emotional outbursts are communication busters, and if we explode and lack self-control, the conversation may escalate into a shouting match. Then daughters lose respect for their moms and tend to behave in a similar way in conflict.

It's challenging at times to stay calm if your hot button has been pushed, but if you want your daughter to hear you and be receptive to what you're trying to communicate, it's necessary. Slow down, take a few deep breaths, and step away from the conversation if your emotions and speech are escalating. You could say, "I need a time-out," or, "Let's talk about this after we've had a chance to cool off." Then make sure you do come back together to discuss the issue.

One little reminder: Avoid sharing with your friends what your daughter tells you. That's the quickest way for her to feel that she can't trust you. She'll be more careful in the future about *not sharing* her life and problems with you—especially if she's a preteen or teenager.

Ask good questions. It takes a lot of attentive listening to ask the right questions. If we ask closed questions that can be answered with a yes or no, it closes the door on conversation.

Open-ended questions encourage communication and sharing of ideas. To get a younger girl to open up, ask questions like these: If you were granted one wish, what would it be? What's your favorite song right now (or movie or book)? If we could go on a trip together anywhere, where would you like to go? If you could change one thing about our family, what would it be?

When it's a problematic situation or conflict, silently pray for your daughter while she's talking to you. Ask God to put His thoughts in your mind, to give you wisdom, and show you how to respond without letting your own emotions of fear or frustration get in the way of listening.

For many children and even teens, the world can seem like a scary landscape. That's where moms come in: to help moderate the normal, predictable fears and aches of childhood and adolescence. Shared time in a safe place, talking, and having someone to listen are often the very best medicines for the struggles of growing up.

Older girls through adolescence and even college years are dealing with so many things: school classes and performance pressures, dating and friend relationships, decisions about next summer and the future. Many young women have told me what they need most is someone to talk to who'll really listen and be there for them. You're the mom to fill that need!

Whatever happens and whatever age and stage of life you and your daughter are in, the vital thing is for you two to keep communicating! "When mothers and daughters stop talking and do not attempt to understand their differences, they create an emotional distancing that is disabling to each," writes Dr. Ann Caron in *Mothers to Daughters*. "If they are able to argue through their conflicts and still love each other, they keep emotionally connected. The give-and-take, the interruptions, the emotional upheavals will not harm mothers and daughters as long as they keep talking and listening to each other."[3]

Questions to Discuss or Journal

1. How well did your mom or dad listen to you when you were young? Are you a natural listener or more of a talker?

2. How open are the communication lines between you and your daughter?

3. What is one idea you could apply to better tune in and listen with your heart?

4. What are your best times or situations to have good communication with your daughter?

5. What's the best conversation you've ever had with your mom and/or your daughter?

6. The next time your daughter is upset and having a hard time talking about it, what is one idea you learned in this chapter that could help?

4

A Mom Who Is Present
and Engaged

> It's only when we truly know and understand that
> we have a limited time on earth—and that we have
> no way of knowing when our time is up—that we
> will begin to live each day to the fullest, as if it was
> the only one we had.
>
> Elisabeth Kübler-Ross

The dark-haired mother in a two-piece swimsuit and black sunglasses knelt on the sand with her two brunette daughters, nine and seven years old. Our chairs were right next to theirs on the beach in Florida.

"What do you want to make?" the mother asked her girls. "How about a big turtle?"

"No," Abby said. "There are too many sand turtles on the beach."

"Let's make a longhorn," Maggie, the older daughter, suggested.

"Great idea," the girls' mom said as they all agreed and started picking up piles of white sand and creating the legs and hooves, the head, body, and tail of a big longhorn cow in the sand.

Their hands dug out sand and shaped ears. Maggie and Abby made many trips to the water's edge to make mud balls of sand and water. Around them, the wind blew, the waves slapped at the shore, the sun shone, and clouds floated across the blue afternoon Florida sky.

Laughs and giggles and bits of conversation flowed as they worked on their sand creation and played together.

"Look at our cow!" Abby said. "It's the biggest sand structure on the beach!"

"Nice!" Mom assured her.

"This is the best day ever," Maggie added as they put the finishing touches on their sand sculpture and stood up to admire it.

Then the girls rushed into the water, giggling and jumping into the waves while their mom patted sand down and added eyeballs to their creation. Finally, with their unique sand cow complete, she plopped down on a chair under the umbrella and popped the tab of a soda and read while her girls played.

As mothers, we have a great desire for connection with our daughters from infancy to crayons to college and even beyond. We may not be able to connect with our girls at the beach, where it's easier to be present and engaged with our daughters, building a sand castle or longhorn cow and making memories by the sea like this mother, but we can find ways to have times—and not just a little bit of time now and then—even large quantities of time when we engage and are present with our girls. There are, however, some hurdles to overcome in doing this.

The Crazy-Busy Treadmill

One of the biggest obstacles to being present is busyness and a driven lifestyle. "We're trying to be supermoms: working, volunteering in the classroom, being involved as a family in church, taking our kids to sports . . . It's easy to get caught in the trap of trying to do it all, and I did," Liz, an Indiana mom, told me.

"But a few years ago I saw a red flag waving in front of me. I found myself on the verge of being overwhelmed all the time.

I taught school, graded papers, talked to my students' parents, checked my phone every few minutes, and updated Facebook frequently. I was paying more attention to my smartphone than to what my kids were saying, and racing around to get them to their various activities was leaving me exhausted."

Each of Liz's children was in two after-school classes per week, and even when sitting in the waiting room during her daughter's dance class, she was restless and her mind was racing, thinking about the next two hours and who she had to pick up next and what was she going to do for dinner.

But two years ago her seven-year-old started showing signs of anxiety disorder and OCD (obsessive-compulsive disorder), and she realized—with the help of her daughter's psychologist—something had to change. They were constantly overscheduled and under pressure. Stress was clearly taking a toll on her little girl as well as the rest of the family.

Liz is part of a growing tribe of mothers who are reevaluating their crowded schedules and dialing down. She and her husband made a conscious decision to slow down their pace of life. They took some things off their plates and Liz stopped saying yes to every request she got.

She let go of the extra job of cheerleading sponsor at the school. They let each child do only one out-of-school activity per season so they could spend more time as a family. The car is now a cellphone-free zone. They turn off their cell phones at meal times and have started getting to know one another again. "I was missing so many moments of joy," Liz said. "I discovered that busyness is a choice and saying no to certain things is necessary to have time with our family."

Wired Moms

The next major hurdle to consider if you want to be present and engaged is the distraction of digital devices. I have a feeling you knew this was coming. This is the most wired, tech-savvy,

Internet-connected generation in history. Moms text and post pictures, they shop online, and read and share advice with other women on blogs. More than 76 percent of women have Facebook accounts. In fact, women use more social networking sites than men, and use them for more relational reasons: to foster friendships, to connect with gals near and far, to share their favorite quotes, crafts, and recipes, and to post their children's accomplishments.[1]

Nearly 65 percent of women in their thirties consider themselves expert Tweeters. About a third are regularly on Instagram,[2] many of whom may be following their kids on this and other online photo-sharing apps. Yet their compulsion to keep in touch with all their online friends is contributing to stressed-out mothers who are digitally dependent and distracted.

One mom said it was very difficult to be present and emotionally available for her baby because of her compulsion to stay connected to Facebook friends. Now that her daughter is five years old, it's even harder to connect. She longs to feel closer to her little girl and be more engaged with her, but she can't seem to disconnect from her phone.

Confessions of a Mom

"I kind of consider myself a recovering Facebook-aholic," a mother shared with me. "For a lot of my daughter's earliest years, I felt compelled to update my status as often as I could. I thought that was being present—sharing all the pictures of her I was taking and posting along with the experiences I posted about."

But when her daughter, Zoe, was seven, she came to her mom and, with a tear running down her face, asked, "Do you like your Facebook friends more than me?" Then she continued, "Would you ask me before you post any more pictures of me?"

It was a wake-up call. For the first time, she was able to see that what had become a habit was actually taking her *away* from her daughter instead of bringing her closer. She hadn't thought of

Zoe's privacy or feelings, but began to think about how she was experiencing her as a mother.

"As I began to post less, I talked to Zoe more and asked her questions about what kind of mommy I was," the mom told me. "She began to open her heart a little more, but the truth hurt. I realized that all she really wanted was real face time with me, for me to play with her and be with her. I'd tried to be all things to everyone but in that was losing the present moment, the budding relationship with my daughter. So, really, who it was hurting was her—but also me. I didn't see this until she had the courage to ask the questions I hadn't even asked myself."

This young woman realized that Facebook also made her feel bad about her own life: Because she was a single mom, she couldn't buy the upscale brands of clothes other kids wore, and she felt sad when seeing other women's photos of their lovely vacations with husband and kids, with captions about how blessed they are.

"After I took a good hard look at myself and why I was always checking and posting, then I was willing to change. That has made all the difference in my relationship with my daughter. Now I don't feel guilty when I look at her; I see HER and want to get to know her more. I'm able to see when it would benefit us to unplug and go to the park and play together. Because I have a real connection with my daughter, now I don't feel the compulsion to reach out for online connections.

"At first disconnecting from my 375+ Facebook friends felt lonely and uncomfortable, but the more I did, the more I could see how much I needed real-life relationships, especially with my sweet Zoe. And now I feel like I have something to give her as she grows up in a world that is even more wired and online: I will be a role model who can be present with the people in her life. Now instead of just taking and posting pictures, we're really living!"

As Zoe's mom discovered, the online world is an unreal world, whether it's a competitive pursuit or makes us feel better about our lives. We have to remember that generally people only show the best of their world. In fact, because they tend to post mostly the happy things, Facebook, Instagram, and other photo-sharing apps are referred to as "happy land" by an increasing number of counselors whose clients are coming in with social media addictions.

When Facebook becomes a place you'd prefer to spend your time, rather than in your physical, real world, or when your kids or spouse feel ignored due to your online activity, it may be time to reevaluate your priorities.

I've seen moms disappear from their children and spouses into the online social scene, where there's a compulsive sense of urgency about being "on" all the time. But the urgent question we need to ask is, *Am I present with the people in my real life, or am I not?*

Dear reader, the reason you're reading this book is because you love your daughter so much and you want to have a close relationship with her. You want to understand and meet her needs. If we're honest, she—and you too—just wants to be connected. Let me encourage you that if any of the stories in this chapter strike a chord, consider this: *How present am I for my daughter, and am I willing to change some things I'm doing and try something different?*

Even small tweaks can help. "I'm not a warm, fuzzy, soft kind of mommy," a Virginia mother told me. "I'm not overly patient and I don't like being disturbed when I'm busy. Perhaps having children later in life and having had time to become used to my own way and time frame is the reason.

"But I've been somewhat awakened by watching others, though this sounds dreadfully judgmental. When I see little children trying to show or tell their mommies things and they're too busy on their phones to listen or watch, my heart does break a little. So now if we are at the park or the pool, I just don't take my phone. Electronics are banned at mealtimes. That's an absolute. If I'm going to cook a meal and set the table for all four (usually only on Sundays) then we pay attention to each other.

"If I am working on my computer and the girls feel I'm not paying them enough attention, their behavior moderates mine. They typically start to act out, and I know it's time to stop. That said, they do need to use their imaginations and toys to self entertain, so I don't feel guilty about some computer or iPad time."

"Hi, Honey, How Was Your Day?"

Lastly on this subject, I would be remiss if I didn't share with you a conversation I had with two early childhood center directors when I was speaking in California recently. I asked them, "What are the biggest changes you're seeing in children at your schools from five years ago?" I thought they might mention shorter attention spans or more computer-savvy kids, but it wasn't even close.

"One of the biggest changes we're seeing is how many of the moms pick their children up in the carpool line while they're on their cell phones. Their preschoolers get in the car and start looking at the movie already turned on in the back seat. Mom hands her little girl a fast-food meal in a bag without missing a beat in her digital connection with friends," explained Angie Colclasure.

"There is no 'Hi, honey, how was your day?' or 'What's the best thing you did this morning?' No talking with their child in the car, no driving home to sit together and chat while eating lunch. It's meals on the go and getting to the next destination as fast as possible.

"We also see many moms coming into our school offices with their child walking behind them, Mom attached to her phone, texting or talking. The children are lacking real connection with their mothers and opportunities for conversation.

"The result we see in the classroom is that the majority of these children don't talk or communicate as well as our students did even three to five years ago. With the verbal kids, we see their parents conversing with them as soon as they get in the car or as they walk down the hall together: 'How was your day? What did you do today at school? What was the best part of your day?'"

Surely we can find a way to balance digital use/social media and the important need our daughters have for their moms to be present, engaged, and connected.

Practicing the Present

I don't like to look just at the problems; I like to find workable solutions. So this week my friend, psychologist and author

Catherine Hart Weber, and I were discussing ways to handle what she calls the "distraction disorder" that many women are afflicted with today.[3]

As women, we have the capacity to multitask better than men. As someone once said, "Any mother could perform the jobs of several air traffic controllers with ease." How true! When our children are young, we have to juggle many things in an ordinary day. Doing laundry while making lunch, diapering and feeding the baby—while answering the phone and tending to our five-year-old's needs—and trying to carve out some time to work at our home business, perhaps when the kids nap.

In those seasons, we don't seem to have the luxury of doing one thing at a time, so multitasking becomes our state of being, our default even in other times of life when things don't have to be quite as hectic.

"What happens in the process is we lose the art of being present and the ability to focus on one task or one person at a time," Catherine explained. She believes that this is a much bigger issue than our digital distractions—because most of us have lost the ability to stay fully focused and present for our children, for God, for our husbands. It's hard for us to focus on what we're doing in a certain time period. The fact that our thoughts are jumping around makes it difficult to just *be*.

In addition, we're preoccupied with worry: Worry about what's coming up or about finances or about our daughter keeps us from experiencing the present. That's why Jesus said in Matthew 6:34: "So don't worry about tomorrow, for tomorrow will bring its own worries. Today's trouble is enough for today" (NLT).

Worrying about tomorrow or next week truly drains the energy we need for today. I love how *The Message* says it: "Give your entire attention to what God is doing right now, and don't get worked up about what may or may not happen tomorrow. God will help you deal with whatever hard things come up when the time comes." Isn't that a wonderful promise we can depend on?

But how can we do this? Catherine told me her sister Sylvia Hart Frejd, in her book *The Digital Invasion*, describes being present like this: "Be where your butt is."[4]

Said simply, it means concentrate on and be present where you are and who you're with. That's the key to being engaged.

Being present and concentrating on what we're doing definitely applies to our spiritual life. When we practice the presence of God, we notice the beauty and wonder of nature outside our doors and in the world around us.

Carving out a time of quiet and centering to read the Bible is essential to practicing His presence. Reading a devotional and praying for the people you love and for yourself helps. Whether it is in the early morning before the household wakes up or later in the evening when everyone is asleep, practicing God's presence will help you be more present and engaged in the interactions and moments in your day.

To be honest, I have found that putting my iPhone in the other room and on silent or going outside to the porch with my cup of coffee and *Daily Light* helps me tune in to God. Otherwise, I'm being distracted by the dings that signal text, email, or other notification. Those things can wait—what really matters is to accept the invitation to be refreshed in spirit before the rush and crush of the day begins. For some women, walking outside or jogging is where they most feel God's presence.

A very wise person once said, "Always hold fast to the present. Every situation, indeed every moment, is of infinite value, for it is the representative of a whole eternity."[5]

Practicing Being Present

Don't get me wrong, dialing down from a hurried, distracted life is not easy. It's challenging to make changes, but if we want to really be more present and engaged, we can choose to do it. Our mental health and relationships will be greatly improved if we learn to live in the present. When we do, we can give that gift to our daughters and model it for them.

I am challenging myself and each of you to start with a few of these simple ways:

- **When eating, savor each bite.** Enjoy your meal and conversation instead of eating while reading, watching TV, or checking your texts.

- **In conversations, listen.** Just listen and give the speaker eye contact and focused attention while they're talking.

- **Do only one thing at a time.** For example, when showering, savor the warm water on your head and shoulders. When driving, notice the vibration of your feet on the floor of the car and what you see around you.

- **Engage in a fun, silly activity** or play a game on an evening.

- **Talk a long walk** to a park or by the water if you're fortunate enough to live near a lake or beach.

The Pomodoro Process

There is a helpful practice to be present called *Pomodoro* that Dr. Catherine Hart Weber shared with me. I discovered it's not strange or new but was developed by Francesco Cirillo in the late 1980s. Pomodoro means *tomato* in Italian, and Francesco used a red tomato-shaped timer for his time-management method. You can use any kind of timer; it doesn't have to be shaped like a tomato. This practice involves doing a task (folding clothes, paying bills, writing a letter, preparing dinner, raking leaves) for twenty minutes, fully focused on what you're doing and not switching over to something else. It can be the simplest of tasks. What matters is that you set a timer and don't stop doing the task until the twenty minutes is over. Then take a break of five minutes. Then go back to finish the task or do the next phase of it.

Pomodoro has other elements to it, especially when used in businesses and the workplace, but for most people it brings more focus, a fresh creativity, and allows a person to complete tasks or projects more efficiently with less exhaustion. And the break—what a great idea! Sometimes I sit here at the computer for two hours without a break, and besides having a sore back and shoulders,

I become mentally exhausted. I am applying this method to my writing and I'll let you know how it worked on my Facebook page sometime. I'm off for the break now.

Engaging With a Quiet Daughter

If you have several daughters, you've probably found that it takes different ways to connect with each of them.

Melanie always made a point to connect and engage with her girls. Her youngest daughter, Lauren, didn't speak her first full sentence until she was three years old. Her older sister, Heather, blurted her first sentence at nine months and hasn't stopped talking since. They often joked that Lauren didn't say much because there was no room left in the conversational bubble.

Although funny when she was a child, the older Lauren got, the less humor her mom saw in the situation. Heather came home from school jabbering about the smallest details of her day, but Melanie wrestled to get a one-word response from her younger daughter.

Their family was loud and boisterous over meals, often laughing and talking over one another. Everyone, that is, except Lauren. She sat through dinner every night with a small smile, never saying much.

Melanie couldn't figure out how to connect with this quiet child. The family all tried to draw her into conversations, but their verbal volleys seemed to weary her.

When Heather graduated from high school and moved out of state, they expected Lauren to pick up the conversational slack, but that didn't happen. Mom finally came to terms that this daughter of hers was as different as she could be from her own chatty personality and her big sister's verbal nature.

When Lauren got her first cell phone, their home became a battleground. *Seriously,* her mom thought, *how could someone send over two thousand texts in a month?* The parents sat her down and explained the price of those texts on the data plan, but nothing changed. They grounded her. They took away her phone for a while. Nothing changed. They were at their wits' end!

One morning, Melanie took a brisk walk around the neighborhood, stewing over the latest cell phone bill. How could her daughter be so inconsiderate? Instead of just sitting down to talk, she sent hundreds of texts!

She stopped in the street as it dawned on her: *Lauren was communicating—just via text instead of talking.*

Like it or not, Lauren would never be the daughter who curled up on the sofa beside her mom and talked about her feelings. That wasn't going to happen. She preferred to communicate by texts. They were brief and didn't allow space for much detail or emotion, which was why she liked them!

"We're not going to change her," she told her husband when the next cell phone bill arrived. "We need to spring for a plan with unlimited texting."

It's been years since then, and while Heather calls her mom an average of one to three times a day, at twenty-nine, Lauren rarely calls—but Melanie is blessed to be on her texting speed-dial.

Mom, ok if I bring Levi over 2nite?

I'm making a blackberry cobbler!

Yay! Luv U!

☺ ☺ ☺

Discover Your Daughter's Love Language

In connecting with our girls, determining their primary love language can be a powerful tool, because then we understand their main way to give and receive love. Your and your daughter's love languages may be very different, so if you are utilizing yours (words of affirmation), and her love language is physical affection, for example, she may be starving for love and you think you're giving it.

If your girl connects best with *physical touch or affection*, giving her a hug or sitting down on the couch together under a quilt to watch a favorite TV show is a way to engage. If her love language is *gifts,* this includes not just material things, but the thoughtful giving of something that demonstrates your love, like bringing her a decaf latte when she's studying for a test. Even though it's a simple, inexpensive gift, it transfers love.

For some of our daughters, *quality time* spent with you is their love language. For other girls it's *words of affirmation* and encouragement, like "I'm so happy I get to be your mom." Still for others, *acts of service* make them feel loved. If that's your daughter's love language, you are a fortunate mom indeed, because she will naturally enjoy finding ways to serve you and others in the family. For more help on understanding our girls' love languages, see Dr. Gary Chapman and Dr. Ross Campbell's book, *The 5 Love Languages of Children.*[6]

The Deluge of Technology

It's not just us, but our kids—we're all experiencing some degree of digital overload in our lives and families. Julie Jensen, author of *The Essence of a Mother: Being Conscious of the Sacred Moments of Motherhood* and mother of five, says, "There is a potential problem when I observe my children constantly on their tech gadgets. There is continual distraction as their phones light up with group text messages, Snapchat, Instagram, and other forms of social media networking—when it becomes too boring or slow to sit still and watch stars with your family, visit with grandparents or walk the dog."[7]

Let me encourage you: Don't let the flood of technology or worries about the future steal your sacred mothering moments or your child's childhood. When she leaves for college, packing up her car with her iPad, flip-flops, ballet flats, books, and favorite clothes, you won't be thinking, *I wish I'd spent more time these eighteen years on social media.* Don't miss out on the joys that you can have today with your daughter and those you love. Even with all the work, frustrations, and problems you may be facing, enjoy to the hilt the time you have, because the days are fleeting.

Questions to Discuss or Journal

1. Was there a time you were more actively engaged online than in real time with real people? What tweaks have you made in your digital use?

2. How present are you on a scale from 1 to 10? Are you willing to change some of your habits?

3. What's your best place and way to practice the presence of God?

4. What is the best way you've found to engage with your quiet or introverted daughter?

5. What is your daughter's love language, and what have you discovered that helps her feel the most loved and connected?

6. Sometimes the biggest obstacle is our plugged-in kids who barely look up from their smartphones to talk to us. A study of more than three thousand adolescents reported that the more screen-time hours teenagers spend, the weaker their emotional bonds are with their parents and the higher the increase in risky behaviors. What do you see as the pros and cons of screen time?

7. What do you need to do to be more emotionally available to your daughter?

5

A Mom Who Helps
Her Daughter Navigate
the Digital World

Between smartphones, iPods, iPads, video games,
and the Internet, being wired is a way of life.

Emily Listfield

- A thirteen-year-old girl was contacted online by a man posing
  as a flattering teenage boy who told her he had taken her pro-
  file picture and morphed it with a nude of someone else, and
  that he was going to post it all over the Internet if she didn't
  send him pictures of herself without her bra on. Eventually
  he had her so terrified, she broke down and told her parents,
  but this was only after she had sent several pictures and was
  traumatized.

- A sixteen-year-old girl dealing with depression recently discovered cutting. She creates a false name and identity for herself
  on Instagram. No longer under the watchful eye of people

who care about her, she hashtags #*cutting* and instantly is connected to a world of cutters and self-mutilators who also use the #*cutting* hashtag. This is her secret support system, as she plunges deeper into a world of darkness. Yet her parents have no idea.

- Amanda, a fourteen-year-old girl, is bullied at school. Her bullies created a site online where they post pictures and hate messages to her. The whole school is aware of this site. Amanda hears about it daily, but she is too ashamed to tell her parents about it, so she carries this hurt alone, slipping into depression and suicidal thoughts.

Navigating the Tech World

These are not scripts for a teen reality show, but true stories happening in the lives of girls in a Bible Belt suburb near us. Two of them are homeschooled girls with really vigilant parents, *except for their daughters' cell phone and Internet use.* There is clear evidence all around us that girls today have a vital need for moms who can help them safely navigate the digital world.

So I researched and interviewed some wise mothers who are counselors, educators, digital specialists, and physicians to gather helpful information and resources for you. Every family is different, every mother and daughter unique, so you will develop your own ways of dealing with her technology use. Yet I hope the material in this chapter will help you guide your daughter. And I encourage you to think carefully about questions like these:

- When should I get my daughter a cell phone?
- Is the phone needed to stay in touch because of safety reasons?
- What kinds of boundaries am I going to set on how she uses the phone? What about minutes used and apps downloaded?
- Do there need to be time limits on her phone? How about where it is stored or charged at night?

- Is there Internet protection or another form of accountability/ tracking to ensure safe use of the Internet?
- Is the GPS on her phone turned off? If kids post pictures from their bedroom, for example, predators can view the picture and find out where it was taken (e.g., their home address or another location).
- Is she responsible enough to follow our guidelines?

As Kristen Blair, mom of two teenagers, education journalist, and coauthor of *From Santa to Sexting: Helping Your Child Safely Navigate Middle School and Shape the Choices That Last a Lifetime*, explained, "A critical piece of parents' being present and engaged today is helping our children navigate the tech world."[1]

The first thing to do is be informed. Understand where kids are coming from developmentally, where their brains are, and what social media platforms and apps are out there that they may be using. "Kids tend to be impulsive, in the moment, and have a great desire for social connection," Blair told me. "So technology keys right into those very traits and needs characteristic of their age." For many young people, even the youngest users, the continual stream of stimulation from digital devices distorts the pleasure center of the brain. Then everything else, including schoolwork, watching the stars at night, having a conversation, etc., seems boring.

Blair explained that while young people love the *immediacy* of online communication, they don't understand the *longevity* of their texts or posts. It doesn't occur to them that a picture they post on Facebook or text to someone can potentially be seen by a much larger audience than the one they intended, possibly preventing them from someday being accepted by a university or getting a certain job, among many other things. That's something parents and daughters need to have conversations about. And always these conversations and limit-setting talks need to happen in the context of a really warm, loving relationship.[2]

In addition, most young tweens and teens aren't cognitively ready to deal with the social pressures of being on the Internet. The virtual world makes it easy to compare themselves to other

I heard someone once compare the world of the Internet to a big city, packed with interesting places and valuable resources yet full of danger for the naïve or non-cautious. You wouldn't let your girl wander alone in the dark streets and alleys of a big city. Just as you supervise your daughter's physical situation and location, monitor her Internet use and teach her digital smarts and safety. While the risks may be rare, they are real and present. Predators lure kids on the Internet with tragic consequences.

kids who are skinnier or prettier, which can lead to eating disorders and other problems. Can they handle the sometimes cruel remarks made about them on Instagram or Facebook?

When Wynne, a Chicago mom, discovered that her twelve-year-old daughter was being bullied online, she didn't allow her to use the social media platform it occurred on anymore. But she didn't just shut down the app; she began a series of ongoing conversations with her middle school daughter about all kinds of technology issues: the dangers of conversing with strangers online, how important it is to keep personal information private, how "anonymous" is really an illusion, and how everything you post is part of your digital footprint forever. She began to help her develop social and media-literacy skills so she'd be prepared to be responsible and savvy online as she got older.

This led Wynne to take a closer look at other social media platforms and why many of them weren't right for her daughter. Wynne discovered she had to be more proactive; she told her daughter that she would check out any form of social media her daughter was interested in, and if it was allowed, she (Wynne) would be included in her daughter's friend list.

Anne Marie and Todd Miller, a Houston couple, work hard to stay ahead of the ever-changing digital world their children are exposed to. "We don't allow our daughter Maddie's digital playing field to advance further than ours. We are friends with her on social media platforms and know about the apps she uses."

Each night, they have an electronic check-in. Fifteen-year-old Maddie and her younger brothers are expected to turn in their smartphones and other technology until the next morning. When Anne Marie and Todd saw that one of Maddie's friends had used profanity with a group photo that included her, she was off that site. They also have a no-cell-phone zone and no TV or electronics at the dinner table, parents included, so they can sit around the table, have a family meal, and connect every evening.

Moms need to teach cell phone safety to their daughters, starting with *Always answer the phone when it's your mom or dad!* Be respectful to others and never answer the phone or reply to a text when you don't recognize the number of the caller.

Several counselors I know around the country are working with mothers and their kids who are addicted to pornography on their smartphones. These are not college-aged kids or even older teens, but middle schoolers—and they are not just boys, but girls as well. Besides the lure of pornography, playing certain online games like Candy Crush can be addictive. Millions of adults and children get hooked on these apps. Recently I heard a teenage girl say, "My iPhone is my crack pipe; I can't live without it."

Many in her generation are spending up to eighteen hours a day surfing the Web, watching TV, texting, playing video games, and using social media. Most do two or three of these activities at the same time.[3] Teens with cell phones text about 2,272 times per month. Even though teachers in high school and college endeavor to ban cell phones from the classroom, more than 40 percent of students say they can text blindfolded or with their phone in their pockets.[4]

Digital Boundaries

Smartphones do offer benefits for kids. They help them stay connected with friends and let them call or text their parents when they need a ride, become ill at school, or will be late getting home. There are helpful things that come with the Internet for adults too: information available at all times from libraries, journals, and websites, the enormous variety of music available on iTunes; Bible apps; and much more. Yet parents' overuse of digital devices can cause an unintentional form of emotional neglect that leads to disconnection between child and parents, as discussed in the previous chapter.

In the midst of this digital culture, boundaries are important to keep our daughters and all our children safe. Be the mom! Although the average age for a first cell phone is ten to eleven, many children are getting their own cell phones and iPads as early as six to eight years old; thus, they are beginning to make decisions about apps and sites and are learning how to navigate online. They need you to be proactive, equipped, and prepared to guide them. This can be very challenging when social media platforms are constantly changing. There are over one million apps available for download on the Apple app store alone.

Another challenge parents face is that the average six-year-old is far more efficient and savvy on computer and digital devices than her parents. And even though apps like Facebook, Twitter, and others don't allow users under the age of thirteen, many tweens lie about their age in order to sign up.

Boundaries can make a difference. Michelle Garrett, licensed counselor and mother, says, "I don't want any of my four children to have their cell phones during the nighttime, including my daughter who is sixteen. They have to be turned off by 8:00 p.m. We don't have cell phones at the dinner table; they accept it because that's the way we've done it since they first got their cell phones in middle school."

Michelle told me that research is indicating the addictive quality of cell phone use; using them causes a release of dopamine in the brain, which is very similar to a high from a drug or other addictive substance. In addition, the screen itself overwires children's brains at night and gets in the way of their sleeping well. The devices are here to stay, so we need to figure out a healthy way to use them.

Social Media

As parents try to follow their teens on Facebook or Twitter, their kids are seeking out smaller, more secretive sites that are more difficult for their parents to find. Thus, many parents and teachers are bewildered and clueless about what their own children are doing on social media.

No wonder. There are so many apps besides Facebook (which most teens today feel is passé, since the majority of parents are following them), so they've hopped to different platforms for online activity, like Instagram, Kik Messenger, Snapchat (also called the sexting app because the photos supposedly disappear seconds after being shared, but they really don't. Lawsuits against the company have been filed because the pictures are actually stored).[5]

In addition to those social media platforms, there are Tumblr, Poof, and Omegle, the latter of which analyzes your Facebook "likes" and matches you with a stranger. How scary is that?! There are new apps and platforms all the time.

Ask.fm is a social media site created and headquartered in the eastern European county of Latvia. With this app, people can ask anonymous questions of other users like, "Why are you so ugly?" "Why are you so fat?" or "Why don't you die?" Several teen suicides have been related to bullying on this and other social media platforms. On one of those sites, a twelve-year-old was cyberbullied by girls at her middle school. Her parents began homeschooling her, but the mean, hateful questions and comments continued harassing her, eventually leading to her taking her own life.

Whisper, Vine (a video-sharing app also frequently used for cyberbullying), Pheed, and Yik Yak (used by some groups of kids to threaten school shootings and for sexting) are popular. A new app called Creepy is exactly that: Anyone with access to your teen's online photos can pull up Geotag location data of where the picture was taken and thus find out exactly where you are. If that's not a creepy invasion of privacy and a tool for stalking, I don't know what is. You can look for these and other new apps on search engines to discover more information.

On many of these apps, users are assured they can be anonymous, but that didn't keep some teens from being arrested when they used Yik Yak to place what they thought was an anonymous bomb threat at their high school.

Until I began researching, I'd never heard of a number of these apps. Many parents say the same thing. "I'm overwhelmed by the different social media platforms my teenage daughter is using. I don't even know what some of them are, or how to begin guiding her," one mother told me. She is not alone. (For more information, start by noting my list of parent resources at the end of this chapter.)

It does take a big effort to stay current with new apps and social media platforms, but it's a vital part of parenting today. The digital world can be deceptive, and as we've seen, dangerous. Boys are harassing girls to send inappropriate photos to them via texts—and threatening them if they don't. Friends coax them to visit indecent sites. A recent Facebook challenge that swept the country was called the "fire challenge." A young person taking the challenge pours alcohol on his or her skin and then lights it while friends videotape the incident and post it online. The videos went viral, and the fire challenge has resulted in second- and third-degree burns and hospitalizations for many kids.

Keeping Girls Media-Safe

"Your kids may be downloading apps that you think are innocent and just a simple way for them to keep in contact with their buddies, but unfortunately, this isn't always the case," says Senior Digital and Social Media Specialist Kristin Peaks at Cook County Children's Hospital in Fort Worth, Texas.

She advises that to keep your children media-safe, it's best to monitor their phones. "Look through their apps, texts and pictures. They may feel that you're invading their privacy, but let's be honest . . . you're paying the phone bill, so you can do whatever you want!"[6] If your daughter is an adolescent, try to include her in setting up family digital guidelines and rules.

You can also check your phone for filtering software and parental controls that allow you to filter out content that is not appropriate, prevent app purchases you haven't approved, and restrict your kids' downloads.

The parental monitoring approach has been criticized for not showing trust in our young people. But no matter how much you trust your twelve- or sixteen-year-old daughter, you wouldn't want her hanging out with some stranger on a dark street corner or making herself vulnerable to attacks or kidnapping by a predator—which may happen when her digital use has no guidance or monitoring.

Actress Julianne Moore was ridiculed in the press for "stalking" her preteen daughter and teenage son's social media accounts to ensure they're protected from the dangers of the Internet. "It's a scary world out there. I'm all over it with my kids." She and her husband regularly check their teenage son's Facebook account so if they see something inappropriate, they can talk with him about it.

"But what about his privacy?" reporters asked her.

"In my opinion, you don't get to have privacy when you're only sixteen! My daughter has an Instagram account on my phone, which is quite boring at the moment because I keep having to look at her pictures. They are all pictures of kittens and cupcakes, but it's what you do."[7] Privacy is earned, not an entitlement.

You can set limits; after all, you pay the phone bills and you are the parent. Those limits might include picking a time past after which your daughter isn't allowed to send messages, or at church, during family meals, or when having a direct conversation.

New Trends to Watch For

"There are scores of girls we're seeing who are lured into being victims of human trafficking through social media platforms," the director of a juvenile probation department told me during an interview. She said that all across the country, law enforcement are seeing a shift in tactics. Instead of thirty- or forty-year-old men posing as adolescents to lure girls on the Internet, the perpetrators are now grooming and paying young men lots of money to lure girls.

"I talk to parents every day who don't know anything about what social networking apps their kids are using or who their 'friends' are on them. Just last week I met with a mom and dad who didn't even know their fourteen-year-old daughter is dating a twenty-year-old man she met through social media," she added. She advises parents that if their child, middle schooler, or adolescent is on any social media platform, they have to know how to set the privacy setting, be their child's "friend," and have accounts and profiles for all the platforms they're on.

Both the iPhone and Android devices have parental settings you can use to block certain types of activity you don't want your young person exposed to. For parents who want to track their kids, there are cyber monitors like Net Nanny, SnoopStick, and Protect Me If You Can.

By the way, the director of the juvenile probation department doesn't tell other parents this information and not apply it in her own home. She has two daughters and three sons, and in their family no data plan or social media are allowed until age thirteen. Her ten-year-old daughter said, "It's not fair! All my friends have smartphones!" but that's the family rule. And even when they turn thirteen or fourteen, she's still had to coach her kids about responsible use of their cell phones.

When she's in the car with any of her five children, there is no cell phone talking, no texting, no Facebook use—Mom included. Dinnertime and before bedtime are cell-phone-free also. "We talk at dinner, before lights-out, and in the car on the way to my daughter's dance class or son's soccer," she said. "We're busy; my husband and I work full time, and our five kids all go to school and sports, so it's important to take the time we have for conversations."

That means that as parents, we are limiting our own freedom for our children's best interests and modeling appropriate, responsible, courteous behavior with digital devices. In addition, being alert to new platforms and to what our kids are doing online is important.

So is explaining online safety and setting healthy boundaries and house rules for technology.

Consider and choose your own house rules. For example, one might be that kids and teens put their cell phones in a basket at night, during dinner and homework times, and that you'll have lots of conversations with your daughters in the midst of warm, loving relationships—about a variety of subjects, including the ever-changing digital world and the risks of some of the current apps and platforms.

And don't be in too big a hurry to give your children too much too soon. "From a social and connectivity point it's better to wait on so many of these technology tools. Give your kids time and space to grow up a little," advises Kristen Blair.

As you and I know, technology isn't going away. Our children's world will only grow more wired and hyper-connected, so it's vital they have guidance from parents. Carol, a mother of a thirteen-year-old, limits time that her daughter can be on Instagram or she stays on it way too much. "I call it 'Envygram,' Carol told me, "because most posts are 'look at me'-type selfies. We have a lot of discussions about it and I think it's good to begin a dialogue with her."

However, some parents feel awful about setting limits because their kids go ballistic or get upset; their cell phones are such a lifeline.

"But it's too important to not engage and give guidance," Kristen said. "Learn from mistakes and start again. Build community with other moms so you don't feel so alone in setting healthy boundaries. And if you're all baffled by the bombardment of new social media, get together and call in a local expert on technology to speak to your parent group," she adds.

Let me encourage you to get your daughters in activities that build real relationships with real friends instead of letting them build their "friend" numbers online. Ride bikes together and do crafts and projects with your girls. Start a mother-daughter book club. (See chapter 12 for how to start one.) Build on her interests. Discover her center of learning excitement. Plan a trip you can take together, even over a weekend. Provide windows of time she

Resources for Equipping Parents to Navigate the Digital World

❊ Helpful site for basic cell phone safety tips: https://www.commonsensemedia.org/blog/parents-guide-to-kids-and-cell-phones

❊ Valuable sites for protecting your children online: www.protectmeifyoucan.com and www.Puresite.com

❊ My Mobile Watchdog, TextGuard, and iWonder Surf are good sites and apps to monitor cell phone use

❊ *iRules: What Every Tech-Healthy Family Needs to Know About Selfies, Sexting, Gaming, and Growing Up* by Janell Burley Hofmann

❊ *From Santa to Sexting: Helping Your Child Safely Navigate Middle School and Shape the Choices That Last a Lifetime* by Brenda Hunter, PhD, and Kristen Blair

❊ *The Modern Parent's Guide,* a series of high-tech parenting books by Scott Steinberg. Visit www.parentsguidebooks.com

can be alone, *without* her cell phone, to think, sketch on an art pad, or write a song. Encourage reading real books and read aloud together even after she can read for herself.

Let me also encourage you to make time for family dinners. Play cards and board games, take walks, go to the park or a movie together, then stop for a soda and discuss it. And have your daughter FaceTime Grandma once in a while if she lives out of town for a real conversation! Since the majority of tweens and teens prefer to text rather than talk, they are losing the art of conversation. The more she learns to develop her real-time people and communication skills, the farther ahead she'll be.

Questions to Discuss or Journal

1. If your daughter is young and doesn't have a phone yet, what are your thoughts about the issues in this chapter? How does it affect when you might allow her to enter the digital world?

2. How present, engaged, and knowledgeable are you about your daughter's use of technology or her digital usage?

3. What tech boundaries have you set for your children? How are these working? How does your daughter respond to those limits and feel about them? Is she meeting her responsibilities at school and home?

4. Does she have close friendships that are face-to-face, not just online?

5. What kind of Internet security or protective apps do you use or have you found useful?

6. What are your tech-free zones (car, homework, dinner table, bedroom at night, etc.)?

7. What idea or suggestion did you gain in this chapter that you will likely apply in the future?

6

A Mom Who Encourages and Builds Confidence

> There are so many hurts that circumstances and the
> world inflict upon us and our children. We need the
> constant reinforcement of encouragement.
>
> Billy Graham

Be assured a mother's words of encouragement *do make a difference* in her daughter's life—it's just often much later when she sees the fruit of her words.

One day a young woman named Maya was walking down a San Francisco hill to take a streetcar to the train station, where she'd begin her journey home to the East Coast. Maya was a twenty-year-old struggling to find her way in life, but she kept running into obstacles and trials that brought discouragement.

Her mother, whom she'd been visiting, accompanied her to the stop. For the past several days, mother and daughter had enjoyed a cherished visit, but now it was time for Maya to return to the fray of everyday life. After kissing her daughter good-bye, Mom said very sincerely, "You know, baby, I think you're the greatest woman I've ever met."

Her mother turned and slowly made her way up the hill. Maya stood alone, waiting for the streetcar. *Suppose Mom's right,* she thought. *Suppose I really am somebody.* It was a turning point, one of those quiet but amazing moments when the heavens roll back and the earth seems to hold its breath. Those few words from her mother filled her with confidence and hope for the next part of her journey.

Dr. Maya Angelou eventually became a bestselling poet and novelist, teacher, producer, filmmaker, activist for equality, and one of the most influential voices of our age. And although she died recently, her legacy, inspiration, and contributions will live on.

Counteracting Discouraging Words

Negative, critical words also have a powerful effect on an adult's relationship with a girl (or boy for that matter). That's because kids—like anyone—move *away* from people who discourage and *toward* people who encourage them. So if you want to build a close, loving relationship with your daughter, encouragement is foundational. If you want her to grow up with confidence, hope, and a connection with you, then the words you speak need to nourish and encourage her.

Despite our and their best efforts, at some points along the way all our daughters will encounter many people who don't notice or encourage them. They'll run into individuals who unkindly criticize, discourage, or belittle them and throw cold water on their ideas or work. Other people may not value them or see their worth like their moms do. Sometimes your precious girl may even be the target of mean words on the playground or be made fun of by other classmates: *Your clothes don't match. . . . You have big ears. . . .* or *I don't like you!*

What's a mother to do?

The good news is that God has given you, Mom, the power and grace to refuel your daughter's heart and mind with regular doses of encouraging words, no matter what age or stage she's in. All children need it throughout their growing-up years—because encouragement to children is like the sun to flowers, necessary for their very life, growth, and eventual blooming.

As author LeAnn Weiss said, "The world is full of people and events that drain faith and spirit from your family, but God has given you the ability to fight off these enemies with loving words of encouragement. Never underestimate their power!"[1]

The Power of Encouragement

One thing I've seen over and over is that a girl who lives in an *atmosphere of encouragement at home* builds a resiliency and confidence that helps her believe in herself and her dreams. This encouragement helps sustain her motivation even for the long term.

This is the kind of home Lana Israel experienced growing up in England with her parents and younger sister. I first read about Lana when she was recognized as the brightest student in her country with "The Brain of England" award as a young teenager. She had published her first book, *Brain Power for Kids*, at age thirteen, founded a company of the same name, and created videos on study skills for students, among other achievements.

When reporters asked her parents' secrets for raising such a brilliant daughter, they assumed she would say it was special math camps, tutors, or high-powered schools they sent her to. It was none of the sort. Instead, Lana said that she and her sister had lived in an environment of encouragement their whole lives.

That was her secret of success. When Lana had an idea, no matter how big or small—whether wanting to try a weird science experiment or write a book at age twelve and look for a publisher— her mum and dad always encouraged her, took her ideas seriously, and pointed her to resources to meet her goal. They believed in her 100 percent. When she failed, they didn't criticize by saying, "I told you that was too difficult for you," but continued cheering on her efforts.

At age seventeen, Lana began her studies at Harvard. After graduating, she attended Oxford University as a Rhodes Scholar and earned a PhD. As an adult, Dr. Israel has served as CEO of several companies, continues to speak around the U.S. and the world, and has written award-winning educational content.[2]

"Vitamin E"

Girls at every age need "vitamin E," which in this case stands for a mother's encouragement. Grandparents' and Dad's encouragement are vital helps and undergirdings of support, but don't underestimate the powerful words of a mom.

The first way to start, even if your daughter is struggling at the stage she's in, is to focus on what God is doing in your daughter's life and what you're thankful for. It does wonders for our attitude if we make a list of those positives and place them in our journal as a frequent reminder. Then instead of hearing what's wrong with her, she'll hear what you love and appreciate about her.

Encouragement means giving someone confidence, support, and hope. It means inspiring someone with courage. It doesn't mean profusely praising every time your daughter makes a high grade on a science test: "You're so smart! You're a genius!" or places in a gymnastics competition: "You'll be an Olympic gold medalist someday! I just know it!" That kind of praise can actually backfire or just not be effective in motivating our girls.

There's a difference in giving a compliment like, "Good job. You're very smart" versus "Good job. You worked very hard." In the first compliment the focus is on her inherent intelligence or talent that is fixed. In the second, we are suggesting that it is hard work that leads to succeeding at something, and that you can get smarter or improve if you persevere and keep working at it. That's a very powerful message.

Several years ago I was privileged to interview Dr. Carol Dweck, a pioneering researcher who studied four hundred fifth graders on intelligence vs. effort-praising, or a "fixed" vs. "growth" theory of intelligence and talent. A number of studies over the past ten years, beginning with her research at Columbia University, showed that students who were praised for their efforts and hard work tend to be open to more difficult assignments and are better problem solvers. They don't give up as easily and, in fact, they really believe they can do better by working harder, so ultimately they learn and achieve more.[3]

However, kids praised for being intelligent, smart, or gifted (person or talent praise) think their smartness is preset at a certain fixed level. This idea sets up a strong desire for them to keep looking smart to maintain their reputation. After all, Mom told Auntie and her neighbors that Laura's IQ is the highest in the class. For Laura's whole life of seven years, she's heard how precocious and smart she is, so she doesn't try things she can't be the best at. If she fails, she wouldn't look smart. And if she doesn't do well at something, she concludes that she's just not good at it.

So you can see why, despite our good intentions, praising our girl's smartness or talent can be counterproductive. It leads to less perseverance and more test anxiety, and can even lead to decreased motivation.

Interestingly, parents of girls tend to do more of this kind of praising, and parents of boys tend to emphasize hard work. This is problematic, because without realizing it, we can be programming our girls to think that smartness or talent is static rather than the product of sustained hard work and effort.

You may be thinking, *We can't win for losing! We're just trying to boost our daughter's self-esteem, for goodness' sake.*

There are some other simple ways to encourage your daughter and build confidence that work. One is looking for *specific actions* you can describe, like, "You figured out how to do that math problem; that's a very good strategy you used" or "I'm proud of you for reading the entire two-hundred-page book. I know that took a lot of time, but you stuck with it and wrote your report."

It's also motivating to encourage girls about practice and hard work: "Your piano recital showed all the practice you put in this semester. It paid off, didn't it?" Or "You put a lot of effort into soccer drills this season. Even after losing the first few games, you hung in there and helped your team win the tournament."

Expressing that you notice your daughter's persistence is also helpful: "You kept working hard in Spanish all term even though it was difficult—and it seems like you learned a lot. You really persevered." Keep focusing on not only the outcome (the grade, the trophy, etc.), but on the new skills she's developed and things she's learned.

It also builds self-worth in our girls to avoid focusing our compliments solely on appearance. Instead of "You're gorgeous; you could win Miss Teen America" or "You've got the best nose in the family," you can highlight *who she is as a person* and what she does rather than how she looks. It doesn't mean we don't tell our daughter what a pretty braid she created or that she put a terrific outfit together, but that you balance it with highlighting inward traits like compassion or kindness.

Our celebrity culture often leads girls to think their appearance is the most important thing about them. As moms, we can help our daughters see that there is so much more to their value and worth. Yes, part of a girl's potential lies in her inborn intellectual and physical abilities. But there are also other internal gifts, even valuable spiritual gifts, to be used for the benefit of others, including the gifts of compassion, teaching, serving, mercy, administration, and giving.

As Dr. Catherine Weber, psychologist, mother of two young women, and author, says, "Always be affirming to your girls. Simple compliments beyond how they look are important. Say, 'You look healthy,' or, 'You are doing well in class.' Talk about your daughter's gifts and talents. How you see them growing, how they could be used. Recognizing our daughter's inward growth and the way she's created can give her hope for her future."[4]

Opportunities Abound

At the same time, we can give our girls opportunities to develop skills in areas they're most interested in, encouraging their hobbies or an interest in chess, music, writing, art, dance, technology, sports—whatever their center of learning excitement or passion is. Finding a team sport early on that your daughter enjoys and can play is just as important for girls as it is for boys—even if they don't want to keep playing through high school, even if they play for only a year or two. Girls who play team sports don't have to look to boys to be affirmed and admired, and they develop a better sense of self-worth.

When I was in school, there were almost no team sports for girls. We played softball and square-danced in P.E., but we had few if any opportunities to participate in team sports. Growing up in a Texas high school, it was all about football and the football players. We girls got to be either cheerleaders or, in our high school, Dashing Debs, a baton-twirling drill team. I chose the latter.

How things have changed (for the better!) today. My granddaughters have been active on the school tennis, cross-country, soccer, and volleyball teams. Caitlin has competed nationally in rock-climbing and bouldering since she was six years old—and still loves it. Rock-climbing, as well as cross-country running, has built so much endurance and strength, both physically and mentally, in Caitlin. Josephine has played volleyball and does Irish dance and jazz, and her sister Lucy is an enthusiastic soccer player and such a great little dancer. I love seeing how playing team and individual sports and pursuing their interests has grown their confidence and strength.

Focus on the Donut

My favorite word picture that relates to encouragement is to focus on the donut instead of the hole. Instead of focusing on what your daughter *isn't doing well* (that's the hole)—the bed that she still isn't making just right, the fact that she missed two days this week of teeth brushing, or the fact that she turned her homework in late—notice something she is *doing right*. A task or assignment she's putting effort into even if it doesn't make an A is the donut. It's a simple principle that will make a big difference in how you relate to your daughter and how she approaches work, life, and study, especially if you're a perfectionist: *Focus on the donut and not the hole.* She needs your encouragement, not pressure.

When we highlight their progress, our girls actually tend to try to improve on their own without nagging or negative comments—and to work harder. Focusing on the donut validates them and helps them feel accepted.

Even so, we all on some stressful days may be quick to go into critic mode. Then we get frustrated and say things like, "You're never going to be successful at the rate you're going," or, if your daughter is a slow-moving type, "Do I have to tell you ten times to get in the car before you do it?" Or your eight-year-old forgets her coat *again* and leaves it at school: "You'd forget your head if it wasn't attached to your body." That's where grace and ever-available forgiveness come in, which we need when we use words that don't build up but instead tear down.

Toddler to Teen

Just think of all the things your little girl has to learn as she grows from toddler to teen, from crayons to college: manners and morals, hygiene and safety rules, drawing inside the lines and using computers. Kids have the computer part covered. Young children grasp and use laptops, iPads, and electronic devices with rapid speed and more agility than their parents. She needs to become a fluent reader, learn to write, do math, and keep up with all her assignments and chores at home.

Your daughter also must learn how to get along with siblings, the right way to set the table, how to fix her own hair—eventually, anyway—how to negotiate with other kids on the playground, brush her teeth without being told, and be a good friend. It goes on and on. And all the skills, and months and years of practice to gain them!

What does she need as she journeys on this long marathon of growing up? Buckets of encouragement.

Yet moms tend to be better at pointing out areas our girls need to improve. We correct our daughter's posture ("Honey, stand up straight. You're always slumping."), her manners ("Get your elbows off the table."), her appearance ("Your hair looks like you need to wash it" or "Your bangs are in your eyes again."). She begins to think she can't do anything right to please Mom.

So let your daughter know what's *right about her.* Sometimes even let her overhear you speaking to someone else about an action or trait you're proud of. I'm not suggesting overboard praise, but balance correction with affirmation. There are times when we must correct, but we can speak with respect and love rather than with anger.

Mixing in snapshots of what your daughter is doing well helps fill her emotional tank with encouraging, life-giving words. Highlighting progress she's making in different areas—her behavior at school or church, being kind to friends, helping you in the kitchen, or doing her homework without being reminded—doesn't cost a cent but packs a very positive punch.

It's also a very worthwhile investment of a few moments to write a note and stick it to her mirror, pointing out her admirable qualities: "You've been so patient with your little brother this week," or "You said you'd help set the table each day and you did. That's what I call being responsible." It takes looking and listening, but as you share these snapshots, your daughter will begin to discover what some of her strengths are.

If you look for something to commend and point it out now and then, you likely will find that your daughter's attitude, effort, and ability to learn will—in time, not overnight—improve. She won't have to go to a stranger looking for affirmation or encouragement because she finds it right at home in her mother's heart and words. Encouragement and support will help fuel her energy for all the tasks and learning she has ahead.

In addition, as we encourage our daughters, they grow in confidence and become encouragers themselves. Someday, when you need it the most and least expect it, your daughter will come alongside and say the right build-up words you need to keep going or face a trying time. Mine has.

What a great calling and privilege to be our daughters' encouragers! As Anne Ortlund said, "It will take their whole childhood for you to complete the job of encouraging [your children] . . . to go into the world strongly, as a confident minority, with their heads up. Tell your children over and over that One walks with them through all this world's judgment fires, and that this 'one who is in them is greater than the one who is in the world (1 John 4:4)."[5]

Ways to Build Confidence

Build relationship, win your daughter's heart, and increase your influence—instead of being a controlling mother. Controlling and micromanaging does not empower a girl; rather, it gives her the idea that she can't be trusted to do things on her own or that she's inadequate.

Have you ever had a deep need to control, to take charge and try to arrange circumstances to turn out the way you want for your daughter? Maybe because you're afraid things will fall apart if you don't take care of them, or you're just trying to protect her? No matter what our intentions are—whether we are fearful and worried, or it's to shape up or improve her or get her to meet your expectations—high-control parenting does not tend to develop confident girls.

If a girl makes a decision her mother doesn't like, a controlling mom tells her how she should have done it. It can be as small as what she decides to wear to the football game or that she did her homework after dinner and ballet instead of after school. It's got to be Mom's way. This mom is often strong-willed, dominant, and deep down, afraid. She may be quick to criticize: "You didn't do that right," "I told you so," or "I'm disappointed in your choice."

As author and family counselor Reb Bradley has observed, "In 'control-oriented' homes, relationships between parents and teens are often weakest."[6] This type of parenting also produces girls and young women who are woefully lacking in decision-making skills. They agonize over small and large decisions and have difficulty saying no, even when they leave home and become adults. In addition, as a daughter grows, control breeds resentment toward Mom, even if she is doing it with loving intentions.

Helicopter parenting doesn't build confident girls either. When we are overly attentive, hovering overhead with too much help, too much money, or too much involvement in their homework, that leads to our girls feeling insecure and incapable.

Rescuing (like taking your daughter's homework to school when she forgot it for the fourth time) "keeps children from developing their own age-appropriate strengths and skills," according to Chris Segrin of the University of Arizona, who did interviews with a thousand college students. "When we don't give the child the freedom to try on her own and maybe fail on her own, she doesn't develop the competency that children who fail learn."[7] It also produces narcissists who depend on their parents for too much and too long.

Developing Confidence

There are many ways to give our girls opportunities to make choices and decisions when they are small. The following are springboards to get you thinking; you may want to apply one or all of them at the correct age and stage.

- **When she's two to six, help her lay out two or three outfits** the night before the school day and let her choose which one to wear. If she puts a top together with a shirt you don't like, set your pride aside and let her wear it. Affirm her choices even if you think they look wacky. Her unique fashion sense will develop as she grows!

- **Be intentional about giving her things to decide** and then affirm her decisions. Read before bed for twenty minutes, or lie next to her in bed and chat before sleep? Have a friend for a sleepover this Friday, or go out to dinner with the family instead?

- **Help her believe in herself.** Let your daughter know that you believe in how capable she is. Give her responsibilities; show her how to do things, and then point out when she does them well or makes progress.

When there's a decision whether to try out for the volleyball team or continue with dance classes in the fifth grade, talk it over. Show her how to make a pros and cons list, and then tell her, "I think you'll make a good decision."

As an adolescent, if she brings a problem to you and asks what to do, brainstorm on solutions but assure her that you know she'll figure this problem out and you are willing to assist. Then you're helping her learn to deal with problems and setbacks instead of solving them all.

- **Avoid the perfection trap.** Driven parents who are striving for perfection often do more harm than good; they tend to raise insecure girls who feel inadequate. If you're too hard on yourself, you are likely to be too hard on your daughter. You'll also have a difficult time accepting failure and mistakes, and you'll overemphasize winning, being perfect, or being at the top. Comparing her to others—her sister or brother, peers, or you at her age—doesn't build confidence either. She's herself, unique and beautiful, full of potential and value, whether she's a late bloomer or has struggles along the way.

Instead, help your daughter put mistakes and failures in perspective. Share a story about a time that you made a mistake or failed, yet learned from it. Let her see you acknowledging a failure without it being the end of the world. ("I messed up on that project, but it's okay; I can figure out a different way to do it over.") Confidence doesn't grow from thinking you're perfect but from knowing you're good in some areas and are capable of taking on and overcoming challenges—and knowing you even have a lot to contribute.

- **Encourage independence rather than dependence upon you.** When you avoid doing for your daughter what she could do for herself, you're encouraging independence. Allow her to do things that will stretch her and that she might even fail at.

- **Think about how you need to prepare your teenage daughter
  and what skills she's going to need** to be on her own someday,
  whether that is college or beyond: from how to do her laundry
  and grocery shop, to how to manage her time, keep a house or
  apartment clean, manage money, interview for a job, organize
  a closet or her desk . . . Let her know that you're preparing
  her to be on her own.

Other good ways to start preparing your daughter to launch are
to *talk with her about issues* you wish you'd known about adulthood ahead of time. What would have been helpful for you to hear
about before you launched that you didn't know?

Our purpose as moms is to equip and prepare our daughters so
well that we work ourselves out of a job. Then when it's time, they
can leave us with confidence and courage. That includes starting
to let out the rope (*slowly* at first) in the early teenage years. Then
later you can let the rope out more as she gets closer to graduation, giving her more responsibility as well as freedom so she'll be
ready when you aren't there to tell her when to come in for curfew
or when to study for an exam.

- **Let her "own" her own successes or failures** and be responsible
  for her own homework assignments, essays, book reports,
  and projects, starting from the early grades in school. Provide
  games and projects that require patience so she'll learn how to
  delay gratification. Don't make things too easy, complain to
  the school, or insist teachers change your daughter's grades.
  The more you over-function, the more she'll under-function.
  If she is allowed to have ownership of her work and school
  instead of your taking on blame or shame because she fails (or
  the credit if she succeeds), she'll become more able to handle
  those responsibilities. Keep loving her unconditionally along
  the way, especially in any mistakes she may make.
- **Help your daughter find things she's passionate about** and
  assist her in setting goals she needs to work toward—rather
  than your setting the goals. If she looks ahead and sets the

goal, she'll be more invested in putting in the energy and work needed to meet it. You can brainstorm with her about how to match her talents and strengths to real problems in the world and community.

• What will build the most confidence is **discovering something she can do well and becoming very competent in that**—a sport, writing for the school newspaper, art, singing, theatre, cooking, academics, technology, culinary arts, or science. Competence leads to confidence!

Where are you headed? Where is she headed? From the early years on, control begins slipping away, but a mom's influence continues—influence through love and relationship, your prayers, and your example. As your daughter moves through adolescence, she will begin to individuate and separate from you. Celebrate the progress she makes toward more responsibility and independence. You'll want to keep the loving connection you've developed and keep guiding her. She will also continue to need your support and encouragement.

You are raising an independent young woman who will be able to think and act for herself and grow into a confident person who can stand on her own two feet. A young woman who can seek and find God's purpose for her life and learn to depend on Him. You'll be equipping her with the skills and strength to cope with life's setbacks and challenges—and someday to nurture her own family.

When the competent and courageous young woman you've raised walks down the aisle in her graduation cap and gown—excited about the next chapter of her life—you will be proud and grateful, even if a few tears slip down your face.

Questions to Discuss or Journal

1. What did your mom and dad do to help build your confidence when you were growing up? What did they do that knocked down your confidence? What do you wish they had done?

2. What areas did you become competent in that built confidence?

3. Who has been your greatest encourager throughout your growing-up years, high school, college, and beyond?

4. What kind of encouragement works best in motivating your daughter?

5. What is "right" about your daughter? What is the "donut" in her behavior, efforts, or attitudes that you can be grateful for and affirm?

6. What five skills or competencies do you think are most important to teach or to help your daughter grow into an independent young woman by the time she graduates from high school?

7. What concept or suggestion in this chapter can you apply to encouraging your daughter and helping build her confidence?

7

A Mom Who Helps
Her Daughter Learn
to Manage Emotions

A mother is one to whom you hurry when you are
troubled.

Emily Dickinson

Jackie's daughter is only six, but there are already so many emotional moments in their house. It caught Jackie by surprise because
she thought Kiley would be at least ten before she'd have so much
drama. But even now it's waves of emotion, way up and way down.

A common trigger is when Kiley is frustrated with a task or project she's working on. She may be overwhelmed as the task seems
insurmountable. Or other times, it may be that she's frustrated that
she can't do it perfectly. Either way, she ends up crying, shouting,
stomping, and sometimes throwing a tantrum.

Her mom hasn't found just one way to deal with her little girl's
strong emotions and colorful expressions of them. But regardless,

she reminds Kiley to take deep breaths, and when she's calmed down, Jackie asks her what's going on with the task or shares ideas on how to solve the problem. Then she reminds her that it's about giving your best effort, not perfection.

When Jackie senses her daughter's emotional meltdown is really to get attention or she wants Mom to do the task for her, she largely ignores the outburst and just encourages her daughter that she *can* figure it out. Other times she tells Kiley that if she's upset and needs to throw a fit, that's fine and she can do it in her own room. And when she's done, she can come back to play. Mom affirms that it's okay to be upset or frustrated, but it's not okay to be ugly toward others.

Letting Our Girls Have Their Emotions

I've been on a learning curve for many years in understanding not only my daughter's emotions, but our sons', my husband's, and my own.

I grew up extremely afraid of anger because there was a family member who held everything in, and then when it was apparently too much, he'd explode in anger. He had a really hot temper. Those outbursts scared me as a little girl, and without realizing it, I carried that fear into my marriage and parenting. Even as a young child I was distressed to see people suffering and sad. I was called the "hypersensitive one" in my family of eight, because if a sibling or someone else close to me was having a difficult time or was being treated wrongly or in a big conflict, I would burst into tears.

I have had a long way to go in processing and understanding emotions. And because I wasn't comfortable with anger—my own or anyone else's—I didn't do a good job of letting my children express anger or helping them manage it, especially in escalating situations.[1]

Sadly, I now see that my lack of skill with handling anger and deep sadness caused my children to stuff their negative, angry feelings. When Alison, in particular, knew I was under a lot of stress, she sometimes didn't want to burden me with her feelings. What I've found is that it's important to express those thoughts and feelings and not be afraid of them. It's what we do with our strong emotions—the action we take or don't take—that's the part we need to guide our daughters through.

The more afraid we are as moms and the more we personalize our daughters' feelings, the more fear we have in conversations where those strong emotions might emerge. As Ali, now a mother of two, says, "When I act out of fear because their emotions are so strong, then I'm not in a place of love, because fear and love can't coexist.

"If we're telling our children that we are Christians and believe Jesus' Word, which says, 'There is no fear in love. But perfect love drives out fear' (1 John 4:18), then ultimately we don't have to be afraid of what's going on in our child's head or heart, whether that is deep sorrow or anger," she said. That is real wisdom and insight; I learn a great deal from my daughter.

Some of our girls might have brain-chemistry struggles and deal with sadness that has nothing to do with you or me as a mother and how we've parented. It may have mostly to do with her brain chemistry, hormones, or genetic factors and predispositions.

Yet the more we trust God for our daughters, even with those challenges, the more we can both move toward health, a solution, and healthy relationship.

Seeing the "otherness" of your daughter, whether she's eight, twelve, sixteen, or twenty-five, is important. This is where you begin to see her as her own individual and unique person, such that her emotions aren't enmeshed with yours—they are her emotions—and you give her space to experience them. And when she does need help, instead of taking her problems or emotions personally, you can journey together to get help. As Cathie Kryczka wrote, "We all hope to feel our mother's arm around our shoulders when we're worried, to feel it gently let go when life calms down. It's an intricate duet that moms and daughters dance—one backing off when the other needs space, moving up close when the unfamiliar threatens."[2]

Another thing I've learned is that moods or strong emotions, such as anger or sadness, are not character flaws or evidence of weak faith or defectiveness. Understanding this helps to shift the focus and goal to helping our girls figure out how to manage their emotions—to empower them so that as they grow up they can find the help they need rather than enable them to depend on us for their emotion management. It's empowerment versus enabling, and there's a big difference.

Different Emotional Styles

It's no secret that each girl expresses her emotions uniquely, but you might not expect such a difference between sisters.

"Grace has a keen sense of moral outrage at the slightest problem or unfairness, coupled with a flair for the dramatic," my friend Debb Hackett said. "Her little sister Olivia is much more mellow." With Grace, a seven-year-old who is all sunshine or all shadow, Debb and her husband use reasoned argument to calm her when she's upset. Olivia, on the other hand, typically needs to be cuddled and made to giggle, and then she's okay—unless she's hungry or tired.

Both girls like to tattle on each another, and depending on how big the dustup is, their mum (you may recall that Debb is British) has several tactics.

As a family, they've had a long underlying team identity, referring to themselves as "Team Hackett." They talk about what that means in terms of behavior (love, respect, support, help). Mum and Dad are clear that members of their team don't tell lies or hit or use words unkindly. "This doesn't always work, but it gives us a foundation to base our family rules on," Debb adds.

Another mom, Sherry, has four daughters in the house (three that are older and closer in age). Sherry told me her girls have extremely different personalities. One daughter is reserved and holds her emotions in. One is quiet and, when stressed, shuts down emotionally. Another is more colorful emotionally. In the teenage years, they had some major emotions in their house with doors slamming, tears flowing, and raised voices.

Even at ages nine and six, the two oldest fought constantly. Mom sat down with them over and over to help them work things out. She taught them about conflict resolution by saying, "You tell your sister what you're upset about. What happened? How do you feel about this?" Then she would have the other daughter share, and both got to have rebuttals. All the while, Sherry endeavored to not let them pull her into the triangle and take sides.

The youngest sister (now twelve) is very healthy emotionally—a really good mix of expressing her emotions without door-slamming. She hasn't quite hit puberty yet, but she hates drama and sees it all the time in middle school among the girls in her grade.

The best way Sherry has found to help her daughters manage their emotions is to spend lots of time with them. "You can't expect your daughters to share deeply with you unless you spend lots of one-on-one time with them, because it's in cumulative time that you become the safest person they know. And you can't schedule that. You make it safe to talk."

Recently, Sherry spent two hours with her college-age daughter, talking about deep pain the girl was experiencing. However, two weeks later, when they got together again, the daughter wasn't interested at all in discussing her struggles.

As moms, we have to be prepared for these times and accept them—to be available and not pepper our girls with questions if they aren't ready to talk about certain things. You can ask a few good questions without probing. And gradually, without pressure, they will know it's safe to talk with you about their pain, hopes, and frustrations.

A Different Emotional Style Than Mom

When you and your daughter have different emotional styles, it takes great understanding and patience on your part.

Carmen knows that her daughter, Karen, tends to not talk about things, especially how she's truly feeling, so if her parents insist, it can feel like pressure. So it's been kind of a dance to learn for Carmen.

Carmen models for Karen what it's like to "own" her feelings: "This is what I feel like if I'm hurt or affected by something, or if I've messed up." When Carmen senses that she somehow blew it with Karen and made a misstep, she asks, "Were you upset when this happened?" and tells her, "I was being controlling or manipulative. I'm sorry." She's helping Karen see what it's like when feelings are expressed out loud instead of just felt and kept inside. During the moments when Karen wants to talk, she's very articulate about what's going on inside her.

"I've had to respect that we're different, to honor that and learn how to let her know I'm interested in her world, but that she doesn't have to communicate the way I do. Although I may like to talk about feelings a lot, I've learned to wait and give her emotional space. I try to give her permission to be who she is and let her know that I'm ready to listen when she's ready to talk, but I'm okay with waiting for her timing. Over time, this has instilled a sense of trust that has built openness between us."

Friendship Issues

Friendship is very important to girls, and their peers are strong, powerful role models—but not always the best kind. It's helpful to talk with our daughters about what a true friend is and share our own experiences with friendships, whether positive or negative. Ask her what she thinks makes a good friend. Share those traits that you think are important, like loyalty and kindness, and that real friends offer encouraging words when a situation is hard.

Sometimes friendship issues get emotional and hurtful, even when girls are young. In kindergarten, Kenzie was in a classroom with a little girl who was sneaking gum and candy into class every day. Kenzie didn't want to be her friend and tried to avoid her, but the girl wouldn't leave her alone. "I love you . . . I love you," she said many times a day.

The little girl also didn't want Kenzie to have any other friends and tried to control her every move. It almost became a stalker situation, though the girls were only five. "I'm going to get you in trouble if you don't be my best friend," she'd say.

Kenzie's mom, Ashley, listened, and they talked about the situation many afternoons after school.

"Let's pray for her," she suggested, and they did every day. Ashley also suggested that Kenzie be kind to the girl but keep her distance. Eventually the girl started playing with others and backed off, much to their relief. At the end of the school year, they moved to a different neighborhood and Ashley decided to homeschool Kenzie and her younger brother, Zane.

Kenzie, now in the third grade, has recently experienced more friendship problems, this time with an older girl who lives across the street. For months, they had done everything together and been great friends, but when the older friend started middle school, she coldly told Kenzie, "You're not my best friend; I have best friends at school."

In trying to help her little girl with that rejection, Ashley sat down and empathized with Kenzie. She shared that she too had experienced times when friends would come and go, and she understood how Kenzie felt. Not too long afterward, Ashley and her daughter invited a new girl from church over to play.

At her young age, Kenzie has already had a few distressing experiences with girlfriends, and they probably won't be the last. Girls' friendships can be great fun, almost like having a sister. Yet often the friendships can generate a lot of drama or bring disappointment, no matter what age. Cliques abound at every age group, and some girls are excluded. Even best friends can be inseparable for a while, and then out of nowhere one becomes mean, starts bullying, or excludes her friend.

Sometimes friendships will last for years—or they can be stormy and uncertain. One week the friend likes your daughter, the next week she doesn't. Relational bullying (in contrast to physical bullying) is escalating among girls; it includes indirect acts and verbal attacks, comments that make a girl look foolish, or just spreading negative comments or untrue gossip about her. The girls who are bullying often lack empathy (the ability to identify with how another person may be feeling), which can make them more aggressive. If there is relational or physical bullying going on, I encourage you to intervene *early* before damage is done to your daughter.

A counselor friend of mine says that some social pain is normal in the growing-up years, but with support and a mom's listening ear, girls will get through it.

When Your Teen Goes Through Difficult Times

Young women today are under a lot of stress from school demands, changes in their hormones and bodies, negative thoughts about themselves, problems with friends, and the pressure and expectations of the culture they live in, to name a few. They are often looking for ways to express sadness and pain. It's a big help when you can be your daughter's first resource. Of course she will have peers she'll share with, but if you're a safe and understanding person in her life, she will likely share with you.

Pam Toohey, an experienced child and youth trauma specialist,[3] advises that when your daughter comes to you with painful or frustrating emotions or is just plain overwhelmed, there are some things to avoid:

- Discounting or devaluing her feelings
- Lecturing her or peppering her with a barrage of questions when she's upset or sad
- Telling her what to feel or making "should" statements that send the message that she has no right to feel the way she does: "You shouldn't be that upset. She's just not good enough to be your friend if that's how she treats you."
- Not reassuring her when she pours out her feelings; leaving her hanging
- Shaming, blaming, or criticizing her, even if she's made a mistake

Some Helpful "Do's"

- Do help your daughter express feelings in a firm but polite way, using statements such as "I feel angry when you ignore me" or "I feel scared when you yell at me."
- Help her decrease negative or catastrophic self-talk when something bad happens. Try to help her turn statements such as "My life is over; I'll never be happy again" into statements like "I may feel hopeless and sad right now, but if I get some help and work at it, my life can get better."
- Model and encourage her to take breaks from stressful situations by listening to music, taking a walk, or spending time with her dog or cat.
- Go have coffee with your daughter at Starbucks or a local coffee shop or go for a drive with her.

If in spite of all your caring and support, when your daughter has experienced a loss, a separation from loved ones, or is under prolonged stress and becomes deeply sad for a longer period than you might expect, or

- if she becomes withdrawn and isolated,
- suffers from chronic insomnia or anxiety,
- can't concentrate,
- or develops physical symptoms like stomachaches or sudden loss of weight,

then it is time to consult with a qualified mental health professional or adolescent psychologist and get the help she needs.

Most of all, be a good listener, and let your daughter know that whatever happens, she is deeply loved and she will always belong and have a place in your heart and home. Let her know that you may not be able to take away all the stress and pain of living, but you'll always support her, she can always share her feelings and her experiences, and you'll be willing to listen and share your stories too.

Questions to Discuss or Journal

1. On a scale of 1 to 10, how emotionally available are you to your daughter?

2. What are you modeling regarding how you manage your own anger, fear, and distressing emotions?

3. What gets you most upset? Frustrated? What are your emotional hot buttons?

4. What are your daughter's triggers for anger or sadness? What is her emotional style?

5. During your childhood and growing-up years, how were you taught (either by words or example) to handle your emotions—to express or not express them?

6. Has your daughter ever experienced a significant loss? In endeavoring to help her through it, what worked the best?

8

A Mom Who Understands Her Daughter's Personality and Encourages Individuality

> One of the most challenging life-tasks of any parent is to experience oneness with a newborn and then to gradually help this infant grow into a person who is not the parent—to see the ways the child is different and to honor them not only by allowing differences but by genuinely appreciating them.
>
> Harville Hendrix and Helen Hunt

One of the great needs of a girl is a mom who will understand her personality and nurture her individuality—a mom who doesn't expect her girl to be a cookie-cutter version of herself, but a unique person in her own right who is celebrated for who she is. That's true especially if our daughter is quite different than we are! Girls need their mom to accept and love them for what and who they are and not for the vision we have of what they are or will become.

This is not always easy.

One day I was driving Alison to the mall for us to walk around, chat, and look at earrings (I am not a jewelry person, but she loved to do this so off we went) when she looked over at me and said, "Mom, you and I are like different flavors of ice cream. I'm chocolate and you're vanilla. Or I'm lime and you're strawberry. We are SO different in so many ways."

Ali was right. I am extroverted, energized by being with people. Alison is an introvert who needs time alone to refuel after being with people for hours. Ali is a woman of few words (like her dad), a trait I admire immensely, for being a person of few words is what the Bible calls *wisdom*. It may take her a while to warm up to people before she feels comfortable and can really be herself. I'm a talker and can strike up a conversation with just about anyone, anywhere. Yet Alison and I both love to hear people's stories; we are both writers and love pithy quotes, great literature, and great movies.

My daughter is super creative in music, is a songwriter, plays the guitar and piano, and can create unique art and gifts. I play the guitar but not very well; I love music and singing, but I don't write songs like Ali does. On the art front, I can draw a Scotty dog and an eye pretty well, but that's about as far as it goes.

I love everything about my daughter, but sometimes our different personalities have clashed or caused her to find me annoying. If you are interested in hearing more about how we've learned to become close friends in her adult years, see our coauthored book, *Mother-Daughter Duet: Getting to the Relationship You Want With Your Adult Daughter.*[1]

Watching Ali's gifts and personality evolve and grow as her life has unfolded has been and continues to be a marvelous thing. I knew in my heart from the time she was in seventh grade that she wasn't going to take a traditional route. I didn't know what her path was going to look like, but I knew it would be different. Her journey has been unique, and I'm okay with that and even celebrate it as it unfolds. How kind of God to prepare me.

It's been an interesting learning curve and, she would say, at times a challenging journey, as I've grown to understand and accept her for who she is, quirks and all, and Ali has grown to understand me with all my many flaws. Have I always gotten it right? No. Have there been times when I was completely bewildered by my daughter? Numerous. And there will probably be more.

Just Like Me

Lots of mothers and daughters have contrasting personalities. Patti West, a North Carolina mom, told me her daughter, Libbi, is very different from her sons. Her boys always liked Mom taking care of them when they were younger, but Libbi was in control from an earlier age. She was more independent and had more confidence than Patti ever had at her age. When she was younger, Libbi was more of a daddy's girl, but she began to need her mother more as she got older. Patti's goal for her daughter was for her to be kind to the world, but to be strong enough so the world would not gobble her up. Yet Patti worries that other people know every step Libbi takes before she and Libbi's dad do because of their resistance to Facebook and Instagram.

Kelly, an Edmond, Oklahoma, mom, was so excited when she found out she was going to have a daughter. Making it to the Olympics in gymnastics as a teenager fulfilled a dream she had worked toward for many years. But finding out she was expecting a daughter to guide, teach, and be kindred spirits with—just as close as she and her mother were—that was an even bigger dream.

Yet it didn't take long for Kelly to discover that she and her daughter are *very* different. She loves Olivia dearly. But kindred spirits? Not so much. In fact, their temperaments are opposite. Olivia is very logical while Mom is more emotionally driven. When Olivia talks to her brother, even though he's older and she's only six, she will say, "That doesn't make any sense. That's not logical."

Olivia is also fiercely independent, which can be a struggle: "I'll do it my way. I can do that myself," she said as soon as she could talk. Having a daughter and doing her hair, helping her pick out outfits—such fun that would be. Not with Olivia. Olivia wanted to decide and do *everything* for herself. Olivia is mentally very strong even as a young girl, which I assured Kelly will be a blessing along with her independent spirit as her daughter grows into her gifts.

Moms and daughters who are a lot alike may argue more. If she's struggling with something you struggled with, it may be hard to distance yourself enough to help her. Moms who have daughters with similar temperaments often think they know just what their girls want. They buy something for her and are disappointed when their daughter doesn't like it, or sign her up for a dance class they would have loved (without talking to her). If your daughter and you have similar personalities, you may dream things for her that she doesn't want. Give her space to think about and discover what she wants to be or do, even and especially if she's just like you.

Moms and Daughters—Different Flavors

Over a century ago Harriet Beecher Stowe said, "The temperaments of children are often as oddly unsuited to parents as if capricious fairies had been filling cradles with changelings."[2] How right she was.

You might be the mom who, when pregnant, thinks, *Oh, a little girl. We'll like the same things and be like two peas in a pod. I'll braid her hair and dress her in lace and ruffles and put bows in her hair for extra cuteness. And we'll go to the theatre and orchestra together.* . . . The reality is you may have a daughter who wants to wear T-shirts and jeans, put her hair in a ponytail without your help, and play three sports a year.

Now, I do know mothers whose daughters have similar interests and personalities, and it can be lovely. Debbie and her seven-year-old daughter, Grace, both love to sit and read. They enjoy not only picking out books and talking about them, but sharing the joy of reading. Grace and her mother both tend to be finicky and perfectionistic. Grace is moody and thoughtful, just like her mom. Seeing Grace's moodiness has motivated her mom to be more even-tempered. Occasionally Dad sees Grace behaving in a moody or negative way, and gives his wife a look as if to say "the apple doesn't fall far from the tree."

"So although this seems to be a negative trait Grace got from me, it's becoming positive because we both work on it together," Debbie added.

Some moms are laid back and their daughter high-spirited and emotionally intense. It can be frustrating when you are very meticulous but your daughter is messy. You may be outgoing and your daughter painfully shy. You try to get her to join the group and say hi to her teacher and the other classmates. You compare her to your friendly older daughter. You say, "Don't be shy! Go out there and have fun!" before group situations, but it only makes her feel worse. Now not only is she anxious, but she knows she's disappointed you.

Perhaps you move fast and your daughter has a slower speed. She's methodical and diligent and walks to the beat of a different drummer than you do. And she *doesn't like to rush* or be rushed. So she often feels pressured by you to speed up. Just getting out the door to go places can make you both irritable, unless you have given her a clear advance warning of ETL (estimated time of leaving). Sometimes even with that warning she is dragging her cute little heels.

Don't feel bad if you and your sweet girl have a little personality clash due to your differences. It is the reality for many moms and daughters.

Even what you enjoy doing may be very different. Your daughter may not enjoy *anything* you're interested in. You taught her to sew in the third grade and gave her lessons and a sewing machine in fifth grade for Christmas. Though you're a quilter and love sewing, she abhors it. She wants to be outside all the time, hiking, exploring, or rock-climbing.

Your comfort zone is a favorite chair, curled up in it reading an engrossing novel in your spare time. Your daughter is so adventurous she's asked to go skydiving for her eighteenth birthday and it terrifies you.

Young and Individual

A girl's individuality is often revealed early on. As Katie and I chatted over coffee one day, she described how different she and her daughter are: "I'm not free-spirited, but more reserved. Caroline is outgoing and very expressive. She's more like her dad. She loves to spend time with Daddy and is definitely a Daddy's girl! They are both extroverts who are quick-witted; it's very apparent even though she is only five."

One of Katie's challenges with Caroline is her occasional inappropriate behavior, not because she's trying to misbehave but because she's very free-spirited and loves everybody so much—including the little boys she kisses on the school playground. Katie had to tell Caroline when she was in kindergarten, "You can't kiss boys!"

"But Mommy, I love everybody."

Someone once said that raising a child who is not anything like you can feel like a voyage to an alternate universe.

Mom's Part

How do these mother-daughter differences play out in everyday life? They are one of the areas that can cause the most conflict but also make life very interesting and humorous. The important thing is that it's our job to get to know and understand our children, not the other way around.

Besides, if all our children were carbon copies of us, it would be a boring existence. Misunderstanding our girls' individual personality traits can lead to annoying each other without meaning to. It can also cause our daughter to develop a wall of resentment because she feels misunderstood, or that she isn't good enough and feels pressure to change.

There's a way to head the conflict off at the pass (a favorite Texas saying from my home state) that I discovered as a young mother. You don't have to wait until you're going ballistic over her intense emotions or terribly messy room to have a better emotional fit and understand your daughter.

Goodness of Fit

One of the most practical, interesting concepts that helped me understand my daughter and her two brothers was discovering Drs. Chess and Thomas's groundbreaking New York Longitudinal Study. In a thirty-year research study of a large group of children, the husband and wife team were struck by how much blame was put on mothers for their child's problems or misbehavior.

This was the 1950s, and moms were the scapegoat for all problems, especially problems with their children. Everything was the mother's fault. If a girl got in trouble at school, her mom was to blame; she was being too lax in discipline. If her son hit other kids, the mother must not have given him enough affection.

Drs. Chess and Thomas identified individual differences in each child's temperament and how people with those traits interacted with people and situations they encountered—all the way from birth to adulthood.[3] What they discovered is a solid contribution to child development that has stood the test of time. It shows that children's temperaments, behavior, or misbehavior, whether difficult or easy, is not all the mother's doing.

Certainly, a mother's parenting style and home environment has a big influence on her child, but what is also important is the combination of the child's inborn individual differences and how they fit with their mother's temperament, and later with school or other environments. Remember, the following temperament traits *are not labels*, but descriptions of different ways children respond to people, situations, and environments that tend to shape their behavior as they grow:

- **Active with high energy or lower activity level?** This trait is distinctive in babies and persists into adulthood. Our first son, for instance, was most happy when moving and preferred to be outdoors. Every day. I pushed him hundreds of miles in his stroller, and when he started walking, he ran. He hated his car seat and was like Houdini in escaping from it. He still enjoys running long distances today at age forty-two.

As an adult, people have often called me the Energizer Bunny; I'm not, but I am a pretty energetic person. In my baby book my mom described me as "born with a lot of energy and happiest when outside, active, and busy." With six children—five of us girls—Mama was very perceptive. Fortunately for me, my first grade teacher was perceptive as well and invited me to help her pass out papers and draw big Scotty dogs on the blackboard when I got my work done before the other classmates. Otherwise, I might have gotten into trouble.

- **Jolly or melancholy?** Does your daughter have a pleasant, sunny personality or is she more often negative and unhappy? Grumpy babies often fuss for no reason and cry a lot. Granted, crying can also be from reflux or colic. Children with a predominantly positive mood later see the glass half full, while the child with a melancholy personality later sees the glass half empty. Remember, you didn't cause this trait.

- **Like clockwork or full of surprises?** Those are my terms for whether a child has a consistent, regular sleeping and eating pattern without your intervention, or if she's inconsistent and you get lots of surprises. Just FYI, this one little trait can influence how easy or difficult potty training is.

- **Fast or slow adapter? Flexible or resistant to change and new routines?** Some kids have a hard time with change and don't rapidly adapt to new situations. In a new class, they're shy; they hold back and watch until they can relax enough to be themselves and move into the group. Others jump in and function well in new situations. And make a new friend five minutes after arriving.

- **Easily distracted or very focused?** This trait is self-explanatory: Focused means keeping at a task even if interrupted. Distractible means being easily drawn away. Being focused is a valuable skill, but if you're trying to get your hyper-focused daughter to stop making the necklace she's working on so you can leave and you don't give her advance warning, it may not seem like a strength.

- **Attention span and persistence level.** Related to the above traits, a girl with low persistence starts reading her assigned textbook pages, but if she gets frustrated with the first few paragraphs, she tends to give up. If she's persistent, she keeps going, even when difficult. Whatever it is, she's more task-oriented and will persevere until the job is done.

- **Sensitive to external noises, textures, or light?** A child who is noise-, light-, and texture-sensitive can't concentrate when the tag on the inside of her shirt bothers her, music is too loud, or the lights are too bright. Some girls, however, hardly notice those sensory things.

- **How intense is her emotional style—low or high?** Does she have small, subtle emotional responses or a dramatic, intense emotional style? The mild-mannered sister will smile if you announce good news, whereas her more intense-responding sibling may jump up and down and cheer. You have to pay attention and be a good listener if your daughter tends toward the low-intensity emotions or you'll miss what's going on in her heart and mind.

Now let's put a few of these traits together and see what combination we get. Think about a baby girl named Sophie who is very emotionally intense and has a melancholy temperament. Her rhythms are so inconsistent, you never know when she's hungry or sleepy. She's also unhappy and uncomfortable in new situations until she has time to adjust. This is what is termed a "difficult" personality, at least when they're young.

Each time her great-aunt visited and Sophie was fussy, her great-auntie called her a bad child, yet she is nothing of the sort. She just has a little bit more challenging temperament for Mom to deal with. She may have a delightful personality once she grows up and becomes more flexible in adapting and more secure in new environments if her early experiences were positive. In time, her mood can brighten because she has a patient, accepting mother. However, it's also possible that as she grows, she may continue to see the glass as half empty and not wake up every day singing "Climb Every Mountain."

Now let's think about another baby, Mia, a jolly baby who is a fast adapter. She smiles a lot and sleeps and eats in a fairly predictable rhythm (and of course has no colic to upset her tummy). Once babies like Mia start sleeping all night, they rather consistently continue the pattern. If we have one of these infants, we can be a little bit smug and think we are exceptionally good moms. Actually, it's just a lot of grace and our child's "easy" temperament traits.

But wouldn't we lack variety if all the children in our family had the exact same temperament? As magazine columnist Marcelene Cox observed decades ago, "Children in a family are like flowers in a bouquet: there's always one determined to face an opposite direction from the way the arranger desires." I think that's the way God designed it. Don't you?

Celebrating Our Children

Understanding our children's unique temperaments helped me to connect with them. It freed me to accept and celebrate their personalities and enjoy them right where they were instead of trying to change them. We need to see our children for the *gifts they are now*, the way God designed them, not as someone who needs to be changed to be more like us or fit our specifications. Actually, God is very good at transforming people, but that's His business, not ours.

More important is to consider this question: *Do you understand your daughter's temperament or misread her behavior?* In the long run, how well children do is more related to the temperament match (or mismatch) between mother and daughter than to her having a certain "ideal" personality, because this fit affects the bonding, connection, and ongoing relationship you have.

For example, there are many shy girls whose moms are very social and outgoing. About one in five children is shy. We sometimes try to talk our kids out of it: "You should really be friendlier. You need to be nice to other children at our neighborhood block party. Say hello and talk to them. Look how your sister goes over to them."

A healthier response would be to not force your daughter into new situations and expect her to instantly thrive. Give her some time to feel comfortable. Avoid comparing her to other siblings or children; that only leads to lower self-worth and more resentment toward you. Pressure and guilt don't help her or make her shyness go away either.

Avoid criticizing your daughter, talking about how shy she is around other people, or trying to talk her out of her shyness. If you're a mom who expects your low-adaptability girl to quickly adjust and master new situations, your daughter may carry a sense of failure because she can't please you and thus senses your disappointment.

Remember, *shyness isn't a disorder that needs to be treated.* Shyness is a temperament trait that many outstanding people had when they were children and learned to manage when they grew up: actors like Julia Roberts, Brad Pitt, and Tom Hanks, journalist Barbara Walters, singer Carrie Underwood, famous historical people like Eleanor Roosevelt, Albert Einstein, Abraham Lincoln, and Thomas Edison. It's amazing how many talented and accomplished women were shy as kids and remained so as adults, for example, author J.K. Rowling and poet Emily Dickinson.

Shy girls tend to be excellent observers and have their own set of strengths. Remember, our children are always developing and changing; those who are timid, with time and patience may grow into confident adults who communicate well. When they develop a good friendship, they often come out of their shells. Those who tend to have a negative attitude can grow more optimistic and positive with understanding and help.

Understanding our daughter's personality takes patience and observation, and a shifting of focus from *self* and our own desire for perfection to learning who God has designed her to be. When we do, we can raise her "in keeping with [her] individual gift or bent" (Proverbs 22:6 AMP), and that leads to acceptance rather than disapproval.

When we overreact or shame our daughters for a personality trait or what we see as a shortcoming, it rarely leads to true behavior change. It shuts them down and teaches them to be ashamed of who they are. Rather than trying to change our girls, it's our job as mothers to accept and appreciate their individual ways of responding and learning.

Understanding our daughter Alison and her brothers' unique temperaments freed me to see them for the gift they were then and are now. It also assisted me in accepting and celebrating their uniqueness—and most of all, enjoying them in the years they lived at home and now in their adulthood.

Let me encourage you to become a student of your daughter, especially in the early years, because the strongest emotional stimulation needed for good brain development is *attunement*: being "tuned in" to your daughter's cues and clues, understanding what's going on, and responding in a way that leads to life.

Her temperament is inborn, but how you guide her and respond to her can influence her personality and how well she gets along in the world, says pediatrician Tanya Altmann.[4]

Let me encourage you to be the mom your child needs, and she will grow into the young woman God designed and planned her to be!

I love how Becky Johnson, mother of four grown children and grandma to many, summed it up: "No matter how different you and your daughter are or how many obstacles she has to face, being a good mother of a daughter from age two months to age thirty or beyond, means observing and spending time with her, looking for the gold inside her and drawing it out, pointing it out, and celebrating it. She may not tell you this, but she wants nothing more than to know you are proud of her and enjoy her thoroughly, that in fact you get a big kick out of being her mom. Even when and especially when she has made mistakes and needs a do-over."[5]

Questions for Discussion or Journaling

1. In what specific ways are you and your daughter different?

2. How are you alike in interests or temperament/personality?

3. How can you nurture and guide a unique personality or temperament trait that you find frustrating or that is very different from what you expected in your daughter?

4. What unique trait in your daughter could grow into an asset or strength in adulthood?

5. One of the joys of parenting is seeing life through your daughter's eyes. What have you seen that you never would have without being her mom? What have you tried to do to improve your relationship?

6. "Each kid unrolls an original mural of mind traits. The challenge is to understand his or her special wiring and its implications for parenting, counseling, and educating," said Mel Levine in his book *A Mind at a Time*.[6] What do you see as your daughter's special wiring and how does it affect your parenting?

9

A Mom Who Prays
for Her Daughter

First, Lord: No tattoos. May neither Chinese symbol
for truth nor Winnie-the-Pooh holding the FSU logo
stain her tender haunches.

Tina Fey

I chuckled as I read comedian/mother Tina Fey's prayer for her
daughter, especially a later part that says, "Guide her, protect her,
when crossing the street, stepping onto boats, swimming in the
ocean, swimming in pools, walking near pools . . . using mall rest-
rooms, getting on and off escalators, walking in parking lots, riding
Ferris wheels, roller-coasters, log flumes . . . and standing on any
kind of balcony ever, anywhere, at any age."[1]

Isn't that what we want to do: keep our girls protected, safe,
and out of danger? As I talked to mothers about their children in
the bush of Zambia, Africa; in the poorest part of Thailand; in
São José dos Campos, Brazil; and in small towns and big sprawling
cities in America, what I heard over and over is a very strong chorus

and longing: for their children to be happy and secure, to do well, to be healthy, to be blessed, and to have a better life than they do. And even if a mother has been far away from God or never knew Him at all, when a child is in danger or very ill, a mother's heart will reach out or cry out to a God who can save.

Oh, how I agree with my dear friend Fern Nichols, founder and president of Moms in Prayer International, who said, "Every child needs a praying mom."[2] And not just in the "foxholes," when sickness, heartbreak, or a crisis occurs (although those are definitely great times to pray), but on a daily basis. Perseveringly, biblically, and strategically praying for your daughter makes a tremendous impact.

- Pray for wisdom and grace to be the mom you want to be for your children.
- Pray about problems that spring up in your daughter's or your life.
- Pray for protection and healing when she's sick in heart or body.
- Petition for the Lord's help in your daughter's school life and friendships.

Simply covering, circling, and surrounding your daughter's life with prayer is the best thing you can do besides loving her. There's never a time she won't need your prayers!

Mother Love

Isn't it amazing how strong our mother love is? No matter what age our children are, mother love is so powerful. From the first moments of holding our fresh-from-heaven newborn to the time we're waving good-bye as she drives off for college and her own great adventure, we mothers are concerned for our daughters. There's a Mama Bear instinct that emerges while we are expecting our baby, increases when she is born, and is especially strong when our daughter is hurting, needing help, or is sick. We just want to scoop her up and make it all better.

But it doesn't take long until we realize that we are not able to control all situations affecting her and that there are times when we can't make everything better. Like if you've ever had to rush your daughter to the emergency room, and the nurse told you to wait outside. Those are the times we may feel helpless and frustrated that we can't fix the problem on our own—but those are the very times that God wants to draw us into prayer and show us His faithfulness, giving us the courage we need to go through the situation and stay strong for our child.

We may not be in a conscious, daily-communicating-with-God kind of relationship when our panic button is pushed or our child's health is threatened. In Susan's case, God spoke to her in a time of great need. She was at the hospital after her second son was born. Her husband wasn't there, and she'd never felt more alone, she shared with me.

"I think the Lord pursued me and spoke to me when I wasn't really walking with Him. When Andrew was born, they whisked him away because he only weighed one pound and thirteen ounces; the doctor said he looked like a drowned rat. His prognosis was not positive.

"It was just me standing there at the NICU glass window trying to get a glance at my baby, and I heard God say, 'Your son is going to live.' That's when my heart really started being tenderized and opened to the Lord. I was in a desperate situation with a critically ill child. He had heart surgery at twenty days old. He could have been blind from the high level of oxygen he received for several months in the NICU. There was nothing I could do; I had no control, so I started praying for my children."

God is so gracious to mothers. Isaiah 40:11 promises, "He tends his flock like a shepherd: He gathers the lambs in his arms and carries them close to his heart; *he gently leads those that have young*" (emphasis added). That is you, dear mom.

I love the analogy of Ole Hallesby, a Norwegian prayer theologian, about infants, mothers, and prayer: "Your infant children cannot formulate in words a single petition to you. Yet the little ones pray the best way they know how. All they can do is cry, but you understand very well their pleading. Moreover, the little ones need not even cry. All you need to do is to see them in their helpless dependence upon you, and a prayer touches your mother-heart, a prayer which is stronger than the loudest cry."[3]

Just as we respond to our babies when they call, God responds to us—only more "perfectly and lovingly,"[4] Hallesby adds. The very helplessness we feel when things are out of our control can usher us into His arms and actually help us to pray for our children and get to know Him better.

The Finest Gift

I remember the fun I had picking out the gift of a new doll every Christmas or birthday for our daughter, Alison. She loved dolls. Her favorite was named Newborn, and she carried that doll everywhere. She slept with Newborn every night, "fed" her, and took her on rides in a little stroller and on trips with the family. And just like the Velveteen Rabbit, Newborn's soft cloth body grew more and more shabby, but Alison really loved that doll. We still have Newborn up in a closet.

As much as we moms enjoy buying special surprises, school clothes and supplies, birthday gifts, or the "just right" shoes for our daughter, there is a finer gift we can give.

This gift isn't found in a shop or a big outlet mall. It's not available in an online store. But the good news is it won't overload our credit card balance. We won't have to spend a lot of money for it or see it thrown in a garage sale when our girl loses interest in it. It takes an investment of time and heart but will yield the most valuable dividend of anything we can do for our daughter:

It's the gift of prayer.

This gift will keep on giving to our daughters, and it will even outlive our lives, as it continues to bless our daughters far past what we can see. Your prayers build up a storehouse of blessing for her and her family. A mother's persevering prayers are vital whether our girls are infants or toddlers, elementary age, teens, young adults, or even grown women, perhaps with families of their own.

Praying Moms

There are so many reasons and times that moms pray for their children.

- Mary prayed aloud for her daughter as she drove her to the first day of kindergarten. Her daughter didn't look nervous, but Mama was!
- Jenna talked to God about her four daughters as she took her daily walk in the early morning light, asking Him to bless each girl, to provide help with the school problems her youngest was having, and for the patience she needed as a mom that day.
- As Karen saw a news bulletin with statistics out about the epidemic of depression, anxiety, and cutting among teenage girls, a wave of anxiety went through her. She sent up prayers for God to protect and uplift her daughter and all the girls she knew.

When you walk your little girl to the bus stop for the first time and she climbs up the stairs to the big yellow bus, you pray.

When she has special needs or learning disabilities, you pray.

When you take her to summer camp, and for the first time she's going to be away from you for a week—she's excited, but you are praying.

When she's in the tug-of-war years and finds you a little annoying, you pray.

When she mentions a concern at bedtime, ask, "Could I wrap a prayer around this?" and then pray.

And when your daughter moves away from home for the first time, whether after graduating from high school and leaving for college, a full-time job, or to serve across the world with a missions organization, and the house feels empty and way too quiet, pray.

Yes, Mom, your prayers will follow your daughter wherever she goes.

The years between sixteen and twenty-six are especially crucial because our girls make decisions that will impact the span of their whole lives, like the friends she'll hang out with, the college major and career she'll choose, the husband she might choose, or deciding whether to follow the faith she was raised in or to throw it away.

We have given our daughters roots. Now in prayer we ask God for the winds of His Spirit to be their inspiration and guide as they journey into adulthood. At every bend in the road and decision, a mother's prayer is for her to turn to Christ and experience His faithfulness and love.

Praying the Distance

If we are going to be praying moms, we need to be in for the long haul and learn how to *pray the distance* so we can persevere until the answer comes. Everything can distract us, and situations will drain our joy and faith.

Have *you* ever prayed and hoped that God would do something in your own life or your child's or family's, and you haven't seen the fruit of your prayers? If so, you're in good company. Countless people struggle with this difficulty.

"My high school daughter has struggled with addiction and I've prayed for her for over a year, but nothing has changed. I'm so discouraged," a mother told me at a weekend women's retreat where I was speaking.

We want our prayers to be answered ASAP. A little part of us hopes God will be like a vending machine: We put in the request, and the answer rushes down the chute like a can of soda. When it doesn't, we get weary or are inclined to quit or at least get discouraged.

However, if we understand that the secret to answered prayer is *persistent, prevailing, persevering, not-giving-up prayers*, then our attitude becomes more like a marathoner than a sprinter.

"But I don't think God wants me to nag Him. I hate nagging!" a young woman said to me at a retreat. "My mother frequently nagged me when I was growing up, and I tuned her out on a regular basis. So it's hard for me to be persistent in prayer. I feel like I'd be nagging God. He knows what I'm going to pray anyway. But I know I need to develop perseverance in prayer."

"If I pray more than once for something, doesn't it show I don't have faith?" inquired another young woman at a conference.

On the contrary! In Matthew 7:7, Jesus encourages us *to pray and keep on praying, to seek and keep on seeking, to ask and keep on asking*. He also tells us to be like the persistent widow who went to the unrighteous judge over and over, day after day, seeking justice. Finally, because she didn't give up and kept coming back, the judge gave her what she wanted, not because he was a good or righteous judge, but because she wore him out! Jesus tells us to pray like this and "not give up" (Luke 18:1–8).

Here's a true story that reminds me to persevere in my prayers for my children no matter what happens: Champion swimmer Florence Chadwick was set to swim the twenty-six-mile span from Catalina Island to the California coast. When the day arrived, the conditions were terrible, but Chadwick was determined. The water was freezing, the fog so thick she couldn't see, and sharks lurked beneath the waves, forcing her trainers to use rifles to keep them away.

Chadwick persisted for fifteen long hours, until deciding she couldn't swim any more. From her vantage point in the freezing waters, the destination seemed too far away to reach. She called for her trainers to get her out of the water, but when she got into the boat, she learned she was only a half mile from her goal. Fortunately, that's not the end of the story. Two months later, Florence tried the same swim again. It was still difficult, but this time she made it. This time she persevered.[5]

There have been many times in my own life when I've needed to persevere in prayer, like the seven-year prayer journey for our oldest son, Justin, until he did a 360-degree turn and returned to God; the long months of praying for our son Chris while he served as a Navy battalion surgeon in nine months of combat in Iraq; and the months that our daughter struggled with postpartum depression after her second son's birth.

But God is faithful, and He never forgets our prayers. He is never too busy. He is never uninterested in the small matters of our life. He hears you when you call in prayer just like you hear your little ones call you in the night.

When your address has changed to heaven, your prayers will go on blessing your daughters and sons and future generations. E. M. Bounds said, "God shapes the world by prayer. Prayers are deathless. The lips that uttered them may be closed in death, the heart that felt them may have ceased to beat, but the prayers live before God, and God's heart is set on them, and prayers outlive the lives of those who uttered them; outlive a generation, outlive an age, outlive a world."[6]

My mom died over thirty years ago, but I still see her prayers being answered in the lives of her daughters, her son, and a big bunch of grandchildren and great-grandchildren. What a great legacy you will leave your daughter as you keep covering her life with prayer!

But How Can I Find the Time?

I know no busier people on the planet than moms. You and precious mothers like you have many plates spinning: caring for children, running a household, perhaps operating a business at home or working outside the home at a full-time job, volunteering in your community, perhaps coaching a Little League team or being a Girl Scout leader, taking your kids to sports and church activities . . . the list goes on.

I've talked to hundreds of moms through the years and find their desire to pray is often woven with frustration about how distracted their thoughts are—even when they set aside some time: *Dear God, please bless my Sophie today at school. . . . Oh, I need to pick up cupcakes to deliver to her classroom and not forget to get Jack's prescription at the pharmacy.* So many mothers are too tired and very overwhelmed. And most of all they ask: *How will I find the time to pray for my daughter?*

So I will offer you some of my best thoughts on this. Because prayer—and especially prayers for our children—is important enough to put our creative problem-solving minds together.

This will sound very simple, but one of the best things to do is ask God, "Will you show me a window of time today when I can pray?" Believe me, it's a prayer He loves to answer. When my three children were under five years old, and my husband worked very long hours, and we had no family in town to help, I prayed this prayer many days. When I did, God never failed to answer. On some days, a neighbor suddenly called to invite our children over to play with her kids, or the two youngest fell asleep for a nap at the same time.

Another place to find time to pray is to use the time you have in your walking around and exercising, in your housework and daily routines. When you pick up your daughter's shoes and put them in her room, pray that her feet won't go to destructive paths but will stay on God's turf. When you are laundering her clothes, pray for a covering of kindness and compassion over her. Pray at mealtime together and make a point to thank God for something you appreciate about each family member. Pray aloud for your daughter when you tuck her into bed at night.

And be aware of how powerful it can be to use your carpooling and commuting time for prayer. In the latest U.S. census, the average American commutes 260 hours a year.[7] There are many things we can do in the car to pass the time, like listening to Pandora or an audiobook. But one of the best ways to use your driving time is to invest it in prayer.

Your driving hours may be far fewer than the average of 260 hours a year, but imagine if you invested *whatever car time you have in praying for your daughter and your other children.* Think what God could do! While it's not the only time you talk to God, the opportunity to positively and eternally impact your daughter's life while you're driving is amazing. God will meet you there. Music can help quiet your mind and even inspire prayers, but I've found that sometimes silence is the best environment.

When you drive by a school—your children's or any school—you can pray for wisdom for the teachers and principal, and protection and peace for the children. When you see a disabled parking sign in front of the school, pray for the children with challenges and disabilities. You can also lovingly and gently pray aloud for your daughter in the car before you get to school.

Here are some more suggestions for using your drive time:

Before you leave, ask for God's help in making the most of your prayer-drive. Ask Him to show you what's the most important area your daughter needs prayer for that day. You may be surprised.

Use prayer cards. I write prayers from Scripture to shape my prayers for our children and other family and friends. I have one right now on the front of my Day-Timer that I'm praying for Ali this week: *May the God of all hope fill Alison with all joy and peace as she trusts in Him, so that she may overflow with hope by the power of the Holy Spirit* (Romans 15:13). I have hundreds of these prayers in a drawer that I've prayed for my children, grand-daughters, and grandsons, with the date they are answered and *Thank you, God!* next to it. They are kind of like my portable prayer journal.

Sometimes I pray the Psalms. For my daughter, I love to pray from Ephesians, Colossians, and Philippians. Sometimes I tape the card with the prayer verse on my dashboard so I remember to pray it when I'm stopped at lights. You can also tape this card to your treadmill or elliptical trainer, or take it on a walk or when carpool-ing. By doing so, you'll eventually learn the verse and instead of being distracted, it will help you focus in prayer.

Utilize acrostics. Another way I keep focused while praying and at the same time cover a lot of bases in my children's lives in the car or on a walk is to pray using an acrostic. My favorite acrostic is B-L-E-S-S. I just take an index card with me and write BLESS down the left side.

At the top I put the names of the VIPs (Very Important People) I'm praying for. Then I jot down what each letter brings to mind in the area of needs:

B—Body

L—Learning or Labor (Career/job)

E—Emotional

S—Social

S—Spiritual

This is a great way to stay focused, and you'll be amazed at how many things you can cover in one drive to work or one morning walk or cardio session. Save room to write *Thank you!* when the answer comes, because it will.

Pray with others. One of the most dynamic things you can do to not give up but to persevere is to gather a few other moms to pray with you. You don't have to be a Lone Ranger and do all your praying alone. In fact, if you are praying solo for an extended time, it's easy to get discouraged and stop. We need our girlfriends not only to meet for coffee but also to join us in praying for all our children.

You see, if you're praying a long-range prayer, you need other women to strengthen and encourage you to stay the course. And they need you! You and your friend (even in different cities or states) can be prayer partners on the phone. Or you can let your kids play on the floor while you and a couple moms have a short prayer time. You can meet in a moms' prayer group that gathers weekly or monthly to pray at a home in your neighborhood, at the school, or at your church. Contact www.momsinprayer.org to find an already existing prayer group in your town or city that you can join. They are all over the U.S. and world.

One thing is certain: Your burdens will be lightened when you pray for your daughter with other mothers. She will be blessed as you continue praying for her. And as you gather, you'll gain the perseverance to P-U-S-H or *Pray Until Something Happens.*

You'll never run out of things to pray if you pray God's Word for your girls. It can give you new direction in praying that you'd never think of on your own. His Word can also give you a second wind and dispel your discouragement when you're in the "waiting room," the sometimes long marathon of intercession.

You'll find verses that tell us not to throw away our confident trust in God no matter what happens, that remind us not to give up but keep praying and trusting God for His faithful working in the lives of our daughters.

Never underestimate the power of a mother's prayer. And remember, just as you don't ever get tired of hearing your children's voices (no matter what age they are) because you love their sweet voices, God feels that way about you, only a thousand times more. He loves to hear your voice!

Questions for Discussion or Journaling

1. A precious elderly grandma once told me that when mothers pray, mountains move. What "mountains" would you like to see God move in your children's lives? They may be struggles in health, relationships, academics, development, or any other special need.

2. What challenges or distractions interfere with you praying as frequently or consistently for your daughter as you would like? What ways did you read in this chapter that address those challenges or offer a solution worth trying?

3. Worry drains the strength and energy we need for today's tasks and tomorrow's—but also our joy. God invites us to give Him all our burdens, worries, concerns, and anxieties because He cares for you (1 Peter 5:7, my paraphrase). Psalm 55:22 says, "Cast your cares on the Lord and He will sustain you." What particular worries or burdens are you carrying that in prayer you can give to God today?

4. I believe one of the hardest prayers for a mother to pray is what is called a "prayer of release," or a prayer of *letting go and entrusting our daughters to God's care.* Whether in an emergency room or waving good-bye to your precious girl as she leaves for college, letting go is the hardest work of motherhood, in my estimation. Can you share or journal about a time when you prayed a prayer of release, yielding control of your children to God and letting Him take over? What was the outcome?

5. Read Matthew 18:19–20. Then discuss or list some of the benefits of praying with other women, whether they are mothers your age or older moms and grandmas.

6. What is a key insight you gained in this chapter? How can you apply it in the week to come?

10

A Mom Who Nurtures
Her Daughter's Faith

It is faith rather than formula, grace rather than
guarantees, steadfastness rather than success that
bridges the gap between our own parenting efforts,
and what, by God's grace, our children grow up to
become.

Leslie Leyland Fields

Children are a gift from the Lord. And now with the aid of high-
tech brain scans that actually take pictures of a young child's brain
at work and at play, we see what an amazing capacity they have to
learn, even from the earliest days and months on earth. We also
know much more about the connections and stimulation that develop a baby's brain in the first five years. Researchers and child
development experts have discovered how truly smart little ones
are and the "windows of opportunity"[1] as I call it, when they are
most open, receptive, and ready for learning subjects like music,
language, math, and logic.

And just as young children have more capacity to learn music, math, and even foreign language than previously was thought, they also have much more spiritual capacity. Children are spiritual beings who have a void inside them that only God can fill, just like adults. They have great spiritual capacity, and with the faith and humility of their hearts, even make effective pray-ers.

I love the way William Wordsworth, the British poet, expressed the preciousness of children: "Trailing clouds of glory do we come, from God, who is our home."[2]

God gives children a special sensitivity to His presence and His handiwork in creation, John Drescher said long ago in *Seven Things Children Need*. He believed that our children grow the most spiritually, especially in the early years, when we associate God with life all around them.

Kids are filled with questions. The average child asks a half-million questions by the age of fifteen. That's a *half-million opportunities* to teach. Many of these are "why" and "how" questions, which take us right to the feet of God.[3]

In the first five to six years, kids spend much time wondering about God: *Who made the world? Who made me? Who made people? What are we here for? Who made the purple sunset and this wiggly, fuzzy green caterpillar?*

As you take time to look and wonder with your daughter, pointing out that God made all these things (even the brainpower for people to create computers and space shuttles), you give her glimpses of His love. As you point out the wonder in a rainstorm, in a bright lightning bug, or in a big bright sunrise when you're camping, you are giving your daughter snapshots of Him and how He works in our lives and in the world.

Dr. Robert Coles, a child psychiatrist who spent over twenty-five years studying the spiritual life of children, believed that children are natural seekers, just as eager to make sense of life as grown-ups are. They are seekers marching through life with an important mission and spiritual purpose.[4]

What a privilege it is as a mom to be able to help guide our daughters in the process of seeking and finding.

Beyond teaching and training is a mother who has God's love in her heart and trusts Him instead of living in fear. For the truth is we can teach our daughters and take them to Sunday school and a healthy church—all important things—but spiritual growth happens through our example and what goes on in our homes on a day-to-day basis in the intimacy of our relationships.

The Spiritual Window

How do we know there is a spiritual window of opportunity? Studies show that most people who receive Christ do so between the ages of four and fourteen, and that 80 percent of missionaries received their call to the mission field when they were children, before the age of ten, as I share in my book *Opening Your Child's Spiritual Windows*.[5]

Furthermore, a global evangelism focus to reach the "4/14 window" has been launched to reach kids all over the world. The 4/14 window refers to the importance of reaching children from ages four to fourteen, an age span during which they are the most open and receptive to every form of spiritual and developmental input.[6] That's a special time during which we want to build a strong foundation and sow seeds of faith into the lives of our daughters.

Like you, we purposed to build a foundation of faith in our children's lives and to gently and lovingly lead them to Jesus Christ as we covered their lives in prayer. I believe with all my heart what Jesus said in Luke 18:16: "Let the children come to me. Don't stop them! For the Kingdom of God belongs to those who are like these children" (NLT). This and many verses in the Bible reveal the heart God has for all His children, and His desire to have a relationship with them and bless them, especially the young ones.

While all three of our children grew up in the same churches and heard the same *Little Visits With God* devotions and Bible stories read at home, their growth in knowing and walking with God has been different. Spiritual growth happened on God's timetable, and each had their own very individual spiritual journey.

Alison, our youngest, had a very real encounter with Christ in the seventh grade. After learning to play the guitar, she helped lead worship for youth group from junior high until graduating from high school. She attended a girls' Bible study throughout those years, yet wrestled with doubt at times.

She always loved Jesus but didn't like the religion, rules, and judgments that alienated people outside the church. She was hurt by seeing the nasty church split that happened in the congregation we had attended for ten years, which brought out the worst in people she'd looked up to. The situation, which damaged the faith of many young people in the church, reminded me of the saying "Christians are the only army that kills its wounded."

The only thing that motivated her in her spiritual journey was the example Jesus set—not a doctrine from a denomination, but how He touched people in the midst of their needs and brokenness, no matter their outward appearance or circumstances.

Spiritual Journey

There is something sacred, mysterious, majestic, and sometimes messy about one's faith journey. That journey is quite unique for each woman and certainly proceeds on God's and our daughter's timing, not ours. We can't control or micromanage her spiritual journey, much to our chagrin sometimes.

Some of our girls will "catch" faith early in life and keep growing without any bumps in the road—staying committed throughout their whole lives. Others won't "get it" until their twenties or thirties. Some run toward God and others run as far away from Him as they can, at least when they launch out in their own lives.

As I shared in chapter 9, the best thing we can do for our girls besides love them unconditionally is to pray for them every day of our life, through every age, trusting that God loves them and wants them to know Him even more than we do. Because the truth is that we can read the Bible with her and have devotionals and take her to a great church, but we can't change her heart. The Lord is the only one who can change hearts; yet as we pray, His Spirit is released into our girls' lives to draw them to God.

Praying for Hannah

My neighbor Carolyn prayed for her daughter Hannah even before she was born. She prayed that her little girl would love Jesus with all her heart and that He would be real to her. "Yet after she was born, I was worried about not spending time in prayer," Carolyn said.

She and her husband were preparing to be first-time parents and missionaries in Brazil. They had a busy ministry and all the challenges and changes new parents deal with. After Hannah's birth, Carolyn missed those quiet times in prayer and reading the Bible that were a lifeline.

"The Lord was sweet and showed me that my new quiet time was while I nursed Hannah. When she got a little older, I would read the Bible with her and she would act out Bible stories. The Lord brought some amazing friends into Hannah's life, from elementary school through college. Those friends challenged her on her walk with the Lord. And Hannah challenged them as well.

"I remember there was a girl she knew in fourth grade who said she was a Christian, but she started playing silly jealous games, and Hannah called her out on it. Hannah told her, 'You say you're a Christian and want to be my friend. I don't play those games, so if you want to be my friend, stop playing the games.'"

Pretty bold for a fourth grader! The two girls remained friends for several years. Carolyn always shared her life story with her daughter. She didn't want her to make the same mistakes she had made. She wanted her to know her relationship with the Lord is more important than anything in the world. And she didn't want Hannah to get caught up in petty circumstances.

Carolyn purposed to keep open the lines of communication between Hannah and her all the time. "I heard more than I thought I would ever want to hear!" Carolyn told me. "We had great talks, all through her growing-up years, high school, and college. Yet I continued to pray the Lord would be very real to her."

One way Hannah has seen God work the most is how He's financially provided for their family in many situations. The culmination was after Hannah got engaged and her parents wondered how they were going to pay for her wedding. They prayed and asked the Lord to provide and trusted He would, although they had no idea how.

As it turned out, Hannah was very resourceful in planning her wedding. A friend of theirs felt like the Lord wanted them to have a "fishes and loaves" wedding—in other words, the Lord would provide. And throughout the whole process of wedding planning He did; the Lord showed His care and gracious provision.

"Hannah has witnessed time and time again how sweetly the Lord does care about us and love us, and it really made a difference in her walk with Christ. He became more and more real and close to her," Carolyn added.

Guiding Our Daughters Spiritually

For all of us moms, it's the little, daily, consistent things we do that will affect our daughters. Lucinda and her husband and four children made a habit of talking about God-moments at dinner-time, so their daughters and sons got to see time after time that God guides and is with us. "Where did you see God today?" she would ask the kids. And in return, little Maggie would often ask, "Where'd you see God today, Mama?"

Another big thing that Lucinda was able to impart to her daughter is how God leads us through open doors. This understanding has proved valuable in her young adult life as an actor auditioning on Broadway. Maggie's had many opportunities to apply this, and when she's disappointed that a door closed on a role, sometimes within days a different role comes up that's even better.

"Learning that closed doors and hard times teach us to go deeper and grow stronger is a lifelong lesson, no matter what field your daughter goes into," Lucinda told me.[7]

Because I have observed the ever-growing faith of my seventeen-year-old granddaughter, Caitlin, I asked her mom what the major contributor has been. I know they typically go to church as a family, but even if they have an intervening event, their teenagers watch an online sermon. I know they are a praying family; they've prayed for and with Caitlin since she was very little. As her grandma, I've prayed for her throughout her whole life, so it thrills me to see her have strong beliefs that aren't influenced by her friends, school, or culture. But I knew there was another element to Caitlin's strong relationship with Christ, so I asked her mom about it recently.

"There's something that has been very powerful in Cait's life," Tiffany said. "I've been purposeful about it, but I also know it's the grace of God. I am fortunate to be rich in women of different ages who have very vibrant walks with God. They are alive in Christ everywhere they go. So I've exposed her to these women and brought her along with how I'm doing life with them."

Besides being invited to go with her mom and friends to women's conferences in California, Tiff and Caitlin love to talk about women and faith. They enjoy exploring biblical topics together and having conversations about problematic verses they look up and contrast throughout the Bible. Sometimes they look back at Old Testament women, like Deborah, who is a prophet and a judge, and study her life. Caitlin takes what she learns, applies it, and sometimes does a talk at chapel at her high school. How grateful I am for her developing faith story.

On the Road

When Lindsey's four children were at home, she read the Bible and talked with them about spiritual applications to life; they prayed at meals and bedtime. But she also practices a Deuteronomy 6:6 way of sharing God's truths with her daughter Caroline (twelve), who is the only one at home now: "Talk about God's truths when you are at home and when you are on the road, when you are going to bed and when you are getting up."

Caroline and her mom have a twenty-minute drive to school and back every day. Before they leave, Lindsey pulls up a Bible app on her phone and asks her daughter to read aloud a chapter of Psalms while she is driving. They do that a lot because it's a spiritual connection point between them every morning in a natural, uninterrupted time.

Questioning and Growing

One trait I love about this generation of young women is they aren't afraid to wrestle with the tough questions: *What has God created me for? What am I on earth for? Who is God? Is heaven really real? How do I know my purpose?*

Sometimes it's the questioning and doubting that worries moms the most. Mothers who have a strong spiritual faith naturally have a deep desire for their girls to follow God as they do. They've invested a lot in building a firm faith foundation: taking them to church, having family devotions, or perhaps sacrificing for them to go to Christian schools and camps. They hear statistics on the vast percentage of high school graduates who upon leaving home, also leave the church and the faith they grew up in.

A Sense of Entitlement: Green Stamp Books

Leslie Vernick, an experienced counselor and life coach, and I were once discussing the disappointment we hear from moms whose college or adult daughters have seemed to turn their backs on the beliefs they were raised with instead of staying the course. She told me that in her counseling practice, she often sees women with what she calls the "green stamp mentality."

Green stamps were stickers grocery stores provided (decades ago) when you spent a certain amount of money. Growing up in a family of eight, my mom filled her green-stamp book pretty quickly. The more green-stamp books you had, the bigger the prize you could get.

In a similar way, mothers may feel they need to "redeem" all the hard work they put into raising their daughters. It's tempting to think, *We were a good family. I did this and this and this. We took our daughter to a wonderful church, we sent her to Christian camp in the summer, we took her to youth group, we prayed for her . . . I deserve a better daughter!*

Besides being just plain mad because she thinks God didn't come through on His part with the "prize" of a girl who followed in their footprints and was growing in God, she struggles with feeling guilty that somehow *she* didn't do enough to produce a spiritually inclined daughter.[8]

Fear-based Christianity doesn't help our daughters, and being preachy and lecturing her on what she's not doing right doesn't either. Controlling her and trying to regulate her relationship with God fails most of the time.

Faith, Hope, and Love

But there is a different way to look at all this—specifically, that there's nothing wrong with your daughter and she's not forever lost. It's a natural part of growing up to sort out one's beliefs and experiences and then decide how you are going to live them out. Growing an adult faith takes time—and in the meantime, a mother's faith, hope, and love is needed—plus a lot of patience.

Some of our girls are very private about their faith. They may be seeking to find their spiritual compass and we don't know it because they don't talk about it. Some daughters are compliant and initially choose to do life and spirituality like their parents taught them.

If you have a strong, independent girl, she may be a maverick who wants to chart her own spiritual course from adolescence on. Other daughters are spiritual Mini-Me's in high school but may lose their moorings in adulthood or change religions after marriage because they had never wrestled with faith and made it their own. They may have been going on autopilot with an empty faith until a crisis brought them up short and caused them to reevaluate.

Hearing statistics about the great majority of young people throwing the baby out with the bathwater and forsaking their faith when they hit the college campus can bring anxiety to moms.

But be encouraged—there is great reason to hope. This generation of committed Christian twenty- and thirty-somethings, the Millennials, from every race and walk of life, are becoming leaders in business, media organizations, arts, and academics. They are evangelists, recording artists, painters, and professors. They are entrepreneurs, heads of nonprofits and ministries, pastors, and planters of inner-city and suburban churches, and they are leading ministries across the country. They are also *hopeful*—almost half of all Millennials across America say the country's best years are ahead.[9]

Here are some quotes by a few of these outstanding young women:

> "My hope is that we become a generation focused on promoting others over ourselves." (Esther Havens)

> "As more young people join the [pro-life] movement, we get closer to a day when every life is protected, by love and by law." (Lila Rose)

> "My greatest hope for my generation is that we will harness our collective power to make positive change in the homes, communities, and worlds we live in." (Claire Diaz-Ortiz)[10]

Pray for this generation of young people as you pray for your daughter and her friends, for God has great things in store for them. He has a bright future and hope for them, and they may well be the generation to carry the gospel to the ends of the earth.[11]

A Spiritual Heritage

What spiritual heritage do you hope to pass on to your daughter? According to Dr. Thomas Lickona, "The last dimension of the parent's role is teaching morality as part of a *larger world view*—a spiritual heritage that offers a vision of the purpose of human existence, ultimate reasons for leading a moral life, and traditions and rituals that weave this vision into the fabric of family living—and our own children's lives."[12] Though it is a challenging mission, it is a key part of our role.

I know I want to pass on to my daughter that she has a Savior who invites her to bring every worry and problem, concern, and anxiety so she doesn't have to carry the burdens of life all alone but can experience His peace. For her to know and experience that Jesus is her hope, and He will never leave or forsake her, and when her parents are gone from this earth into eternity she *always* has a refuge in the heart of God, her Creator, who loves her with a forever love. And that life with Jesus, discovering the purpose He has for her, following it and letting Him use her gifts wherever He leads her—is a great adventure—in fact, the greatest adventure on earth.

What do you want to pass along to your daughter spiritually?

As Jim Burns, youth and family specialist, said, "Remember that your words are important, but they can only go so far. So much of the work of passing on a legacy of faith takes place when we model it ourselves and believe in our children." Children do learn what we live, especially spiritually!

To pass on a legacy of faith in God, Jim says, "We must make sure that we as parents are working on these same issues within our own lives. It will take a plan, intentionality, and help from above. But I believe you can lead the way for your children and make a generational difference for lifetimes to come."[13]

Remember that the most contagious faith is a joyful, grace-filled faith that you live out before your daughter throughout her years at home. It's being a steppingstone to Christ instead of a stumbling block. It's your daughter seeing that her mom has a real relationship with a living God whom *she knows* (instead of just knows about) and *she hears* (instead of just hears about what God used to do in the Bible days). And that it's important to us to help her know God, and to listen and hear God for herself.

Wherever your daughter is regarding her faith right now—whether she is running toward God or away from Him, or is somewhere in the middle, is apathetic or seemingly not interested—and wherever she may journey in the future—let me encourage you to *never stop praying for her*. Keep believing that God is able to fulfill His purposes and weave His plan for good into her life. Keep hoping and praying and trusting that He will complete His work in her, and that through His mighty power at work within her, "[He] is able . . . to accomplish infinitely more than we might ask or think" (Ephesians 3:20–21 NLT).

Questions to Discuss or Journal

1. Describe your faith when you were your daughter's present age.

2. It helps tremendously to remember when you had a spiritual awakening or spiritual reconnection with God as an adult. What was the process, people, or situations that led you to a closer, more committed relationship with Christ?

3. How did your mom react or respond to you if you had a different spiritual journey than she expected? Was she a steppingstone or a stumbling block?

4. Regarding your daughter's faith journey, what are you most grateful for? What are your concerns or worries for your daughter right now? What, if anything, is she struggling with? Write each one down and pray about them with a trusted friend.

5. Where are you and God right now? Draw a picture of how you feel about the Lord and how you think He feels about you, and discuss it with someone.

6. What do you want to pass on to your daughter as a spiritual legacy that she can take through life and perhaps pass on to her children?

11

A Mom Who Is a
Good Role Model

Parenting, including the moral standards we teach
and uphold, has a profound impact on our children's
moral development and behavior. When we do not
set high standards, we abandon our kids to their
immature desires and the negative pressures of the
peer group and culture.

Dr. Thomas Lickona

I was visiting at a neighbor's house one day when her five-year-
old suddenly put her hands on her hips, pointed her finger at her
brother who had just thrown a truck across the room, and said
firmly, "You'll just have to go to time-out *right now!*" My neighbor
chuckled as she realized how much her daughter sounded just like
she did—facial expression, words, and all. She was observing Mom
all the time, even when Mom wasn't aware of it.

Have you ever seen your daughter mirror your behavior or talk?
Like the time you said a not-very-nice word when another car cut

you off in traffic or when you lost your temper because mud was tracked onto your white carpet by the dog? Or, on a positive note, when your little sweetheart mirrored your generosity by sharing half her sandwich with a girl at the lunch table because she didn't have a lunch?

Our children have in their toolboxes very good tape recorders and video cameras, stronger than any digital recording device on earth. They are listening and recording when we least expect it. As an older friend once told me, "Kids seldom misquote you. They more often repeat word for word what you shouldn't have said."

The Impact of Our Example

A primary need girls have today is moms who are good role models. We may not feel like we're worthy to be of great influence, but because the major way children learn between right and wrong is by watching adults, you have a great opportunity to influence her. As you lead by example, the "modeling" you do is more effective and powerful than any lectures, teaching, and advice can ever be. Live as if your girls are watching, Mom, because they are!

When my children were young, I was very struck by the following poem, and the daunting nature of parenting sunk in even more deeply as I read the words a second time. I still find it a wonderful reminder of the truth that our daughters' ears are listening and their eyes are watching all we do (as are your sons').

> There are little eyes upon you,
> And they are watching night and day;
> There are little ears that quickly
> Take in every word you say.
>
> There are little hands all eager
> To do everything you do;
> And a little girl who's dreaming
> of the day she'll be like you.

You're the sweetheart's idol;
You're the wisest of the wise;
In her little mind, about you
No suspicions ever rise.

She believes in you devotedly;
Holds that all you say and do,
She will say and do in your way
When she's grown up just like you.

There's a wide-eyed little sweetheart
Who believes you're always right;
And her ears are always open,
And she watches day and night.

You are setting an example
Every day in all you do;
For the little child who's waiting
To grow up to be like you.[1]

Edgar Guest, 1881–1959

Whatever the issue is—smoking, alcohol or drug use, seat belt use, television viewing habits, digital and cell phone habits, table manners—did you know that a mother's example is more powerful than a celebrity's nationwide campaign, that kids are more influenced by their mother's actions than anyone else's influence? Studies show the main factor that determines whether children say yes or no to the above substances or habits is their parents' example, *especially their mothers.* Our girls will assume it is okay to do whatever they see you do or say. In doing so, they unconsciously internalize the behavior and values you live by.

We all know that one's example can influence children for the positive or the negative, depending on what is being modeled. Dads have a very big impact on children, and so do grandparents, siblings, peers, teachers, and movie and sports stars. We can also encourage our daughters to look for positive role models at school and in sports.

However, girls are especially perceptive to what their mothers do, how we deal with difficulties. Whether we panic as if every problem is a crisis or whether we handle those situations as opportunities. Whether we limit usage of digital connection to make time for person-to-person interaction. Whether we are active or sedentary, grateful or complaining, unhappy or fairly content on a regular basis. If we are overly critical toward ourselves and others, this teaches our girls to be overly critical toward themselves and others as well.

How do we pass on a sense of humor, vital for living and surviving in a tough and stressful world? Usually by example, and maybe through some of our genes as well. As Becky, a Colorado mom I know, says, "One thing I have passed down to my daughter, above all else perhaps, is the ability to look, find, tell, and retell the funny things in life in a story. Humor is a gift handed down in our family; the females in our family tree could have given Lucille Ball, Carol Burnett, and Tina Fey a run for their money. It is so fun to see my daughter blossom in her comedic style."

As parents, we can lose our sense of humor. We can become so serious or feel like the world is on our shoulders, especially on difficult days. Yet sharing laughter with our kids, friends, and spouse connects us. It reduces stress and helps our mental and physical health. Being playful or silly, playing a game just for fun, or watching a funny movie can help revive our sense of humor.

As Steven W. Vannoy said, "Without a sense of humor, life can be colorless, a terrible burden. With it, we enjoy the process of living. We have more joy to share with others."[2]

Kindness and Empathy Are Contagious

Our daughters also observe how we deal with relationships, whether we treat our husband, neighbor, or the grocery checker with kindness or are in such a hurry we rush brusquely by them, criticize, or mistreat them. They notice when we make dinner for a family in the neighborhood whose mother has been sick, and they enjoy helping us deliver it.

Here are some kindnesses that may inspire your daughter to empathy and perhaps want to join you:

- Gather the contents for and send a care package to a deployed or wounded military person.
- Give a disposable glass of iced tea or lemonade to your postal carrier on a hot day or hot cocoa on a cold day.
- Give someone a compliment, which can brighten their day.
- Write a thank-you note to someone whose help made a difference.
- Collect Box Tops (from literally hundreds of products) and contribute to a local elementary school, even if your children don't attend there. See www.boxtops4education.com to check which schools around you participate.

What Our Daughters Learn

Our girls especially watch what we eat and record in their smart brains what we think and say about our bodies and weight. Along the way, they tend to learn and imitate our behavior, lifestyle patterns, words, and attitudes. They watch how we take care of ourselves and how we view ourselves, even during their early years.

As they go through elementary, middle school, and beyond, girls are bombarded with airbrushed, photoshopped, body-double images and ideals that are nearly impossible to achieve. Our daughters are most at risk, and you play a crucial role in how your girl views herself and takes care of herself, and what she expects of herself.

With all they are exposed to these days, girls' thoughts can run wild with issues of lack of confidence, depression, fears about their bodies or physical, hormonal, or emotional changes going on. "If they're alone with these thoughts for very long and the primary influence is friends and social media, all the wrong things about their importance and identity are going to be reinforced," says Michelle Garrett, a licensed counselor.

"What we teach our girls and how we live our lives needs to be consistent. How I treat myself and my body sends powerful messages to my daughter. If I care for everyone else but not myself, what am I showing her day in and day out? What will become the important attributes that she takes in and makes her own?"[3] (This is why I've devoted chapter 14 to how we can help our daughters develop a healthy body image and nurture their femininity.)

With these and other issues, as we think about girls learning values through seeing you model them, think of all the many opportunities there are every day to help guide and influence your daughter. Just by the way you live, love, and carry on your daily life you can make a big difference in her life.

Though we want to be good examples for our daughters, the truth is, despite all our best efforts and intentions, we can't ever be the perfect role models or the perfect moms.

In fact, as I have shared before, we don't need to aim for perfection in our parenting. "Perfectionism never happens in a vacuum. It touches everyone around us," says research professor Brené Brown in *The Gifts of Imperfection*. "We pass it down to our children, we infect our workplace with impossible expectations, and it's suffocating for our friends and families. Thankfully, compassion also spreads quickly. When we're kind to ourselves, we create a reservoir of compassion that we can extend to others. Our children learn how to be self-compassionate by watching us, and the people around us feel free to be authentic and connected."[4]

We will all blow it or have bad days, say or do things in the heat of frustration we wish later we could erase. That's where grace comes in. And forgiveness. And second and even third chances. We need regular doses of God's grace to be the moms we want to be for our girls. And saying "I'm sorry" and "Forgive me" when we fail or hurt someone provides a great example of humility.

Connectedness and the Family

Elayne Bennett has written an important book called *Daughters in Danger: Helping Our Girls Thrive in Today's Culture,*[5] in which she discusses the dangers and challenges that our girls face in the moral climate they are immersed in today. "Teenagers are famously cynical. They cannot be told how to behave, at least not successfully. They have to absorb life's lessons from what they experience. There is no better place to learn than at home, and no people are more capable of imparting those lessons than a girl's parents." Bennett's book is a must-read for parents, educators, and physicians to help them understand what girls are facing in this toxic culture and then offers tools to help them.

Elayne cites a $25 million longitudinal study of adolescents known as "Add Health" that confirms the importance of the home, parental guidance, and role models in the lives of young people. Twenty thousand teenagers from all over the country and all backgrounds and their parents were interviewed and tracked over time. Over four thousand journal articles have been written about the outcomes and discoveries from the Add Health's studies.[6]

One piece of evidence is that girls, for a number of reasons, are having sex before they are ready. Dr. Meg Meeker explained, "Basically, teens are having sex to find something missing in their lives." Dr. Meeker believes what is most often missing is a connection with their parents—connectedness that starts with getting to know the world our daughters inhabit, both in real life and online.[7]

Another important finding concerning the importance of Mom and Dad comes from the study's lead researcher, Michael D. Resnick, who wrote, "Teenagers who bond with loving, caring parents are far more likely to avoid high-risk behaviors, sex included, than their peers."[8]

Susan Vogt, author of *Raising Kids Who Make a Difference*, did a survey with many young adults, asking them what influenced them to say no to drugs now and when they were teens. Besides the fact that their parents built a strong enough self-respect in their kids that they weren't easily led, the major themes and reasons these young adults reported are very helpful to consider:

- Model your belief. "My parents didn't smoke or abuse alcohol."
- Lead a full life. "I had plenty of other interesting things to do."
- Pick good friends. "None of my friends were doing it."
- Take a stand. "Teachers took a clear stand against substance abuse and explained why it was bad."
- Have a purpose in life. "I had a bigger goal in life that kept me focused."

Building Trust

Our granddaughter Caitlin has had good role models in her home—her mom and dad—along with close and trusting relationships. She also has the role models of vibrant Christian women around her that she looks up to and who mentor her.

But the relationship she and her mom have is special. "While Mom will let me express myself and let me be adventurous in my rock-climbing competitions, I have to earn her trust," she told me. "So growing up and even now, I have been careful about what I do and think about situations I'm in because I don't want to misplace or betray her trust.

"I could go out and drink, but I don't. I could go see an R-rated movie or watch an R-rated movie at my friend's house, but I don't. I take the initiative to show her I'm trustworthy. She trusts me and I know it. I think it's that trust that has helped motivate me to do the right thing.

"When I took driver's training, Mom and Dad let me drive because they knew I'd be responsible about it. All through middle school and high school, I didn't do stupid things. I don't do drugs, smoke, or drink. I've had many opportunities, but I chose not to. All the health classes helped because I know what smoking does to your lungs. Mom knows my thought processes and we talk about things."[9]

Caitlin has learned important life lessons through her parents' role-modeling and life: a deep faith in God, communication skills and conflict resolution; living with purpose; hospitality; loving God, family, and friends . . . I'm so glad that Tiff is Caitlin and Caleb's mother and that I get to be her Nandy, the grandma name she gave me when she was a toddler.

Questions to Discuss or Journal

1. Who were your favorite or most influential role models when you were growing up? What impact did they have on you?

2. What are the five major values that shape and guide your life?

3. What kinds of pressures is your daughter facing?

4. What is the center of your home, the place where you all gather and spend the most time?

5. How are you modeling kindness and compassion?

6. In what ways are you modeling faith in God? How does your daughter respond and what are the other spiritual influences in her life?

12

A Mom Who Fosters
Her Daughter's Learning

Every one of us needs education to help us shine our dreams! And that is why I believe education should be one of our dreams.

Heather Whitestone McCallum,
Miss America 1995

"What does *bilious* mean, Mom?" Alison asked years ago when she was reading *A Wrinkle in Time* by Madeleine L'Engle. Propped up in bed, she was at home sick with a bout of bronchitis.

"I don't know off the top of my head, but let me get the dictionary and we'll see," I replied, heading down the hall with an armful of laundry. A few minutes later I brought our copy of *Webster's Dictionary* to Ali's bedside and we looked up the word: "bilious: (a) relating to bile, (b) disagreeable, bad-tempered."

Then she read me the sentence the word appeared in, and suddenly the light went on. She understood the meaning of *bilious* in the context of the story. A few pages later she asked, "What about *sinister?*" but before I could answer, Alison said, "I'll look that one up!" and picked up the dictionary to find and read it aloud.

Besides providing an opportunity for vocabulary building, when we say, "Let's look it up," we make use of a positive, very inexpensive way of fanning the flame of learning and curiosity in our girls. Curiosity is important because it is what fuels motivation for learning. When curiosity dies, motivation fades.

So whether it's a question about the meaning of a word, a faraway, newly discovered constellation, a political issue, or an obscure historical fact, when you show that you care enough to investigate with your daughter—that you too are curious and like to learn— your girl will pick up that learning isn't just all about worksheets, homework, and tests. When you encourage her to question, wonder, and think critically, what is transferred to her is that learning is an exciting and lifelong pursuit.

When she does ask a question you have no idea about, nor the time to pursue in that moment, it's helpful to keep a stack of index cards on your kitchen counter and a few in your purse. Write the question down and later go to the library together. It's a simple but powerful way to show her—without words—that intellectual curiosity is important and her questions are valuable enough to pursue.

Asking "What do you think?" instead of giving her an answer, before or after you read a paragraph together that zeroes in on the information, can be a great confidence-builder.

And yes, you can Google the question and answer! The Internet is such a handy tool for searching information at any time or place. You thought I forgot that we are in the twenty-first century—but no! I often look up things online. I look up historical people's biographies and historical events after we see a movie or documentary about them. I search for and read about political issues and read reviews before we go see a movie or I buy a new book. I also search out the best ways to prune our knockout rosebushes or create a gluten-free Thanksgiving dinner.

But there's nothing like pursuing information, searching for a person, concept, scientific principle, or definition of a fascinating word, in a real book.

And remember, one of the most powerful and painless things you can do to boost your daughter's love of reading just by the way you live is to let her see you totally enthralled in a novel. Let her hear you chuckle as you read a political cartoon in the newspaper. Nothing is as motivating for a girl as watching her mom caught in the act of sheer enjoyment while reading a story or novel. She'll sense the magic of reading even before she's learned to decode words, and it will stay with her.

"Thank You, Mom"

When Ann was in her first year of college, she wrote her mother a letter telling her how grateful she was for the classics, poetry, Scripture, and great literature she and her siblings were required to read at home. Much of it they read aloud together in the evening or read on their own and wrote book reports about.

That's not what Ann had always thought about all the extra reading her mother assigned. But her mom, Susan, knew the students rarely read the classics in public schools and thought they were often assigned mediocre "age-appropriate" reading that wasn't challenging enough. So she developed her own must-read list for her daughters and son. She started with reading aloud Beatrix Potter and A. A. Milne books to her young children, along with the Madeline books, *Peter Pan, The Velveteen Rabbit*, and other classics.

Later Susan discovered that if she wanted her children to read great books like *Little Women, Five Little Peppers, Ivanhoe, Tom Sawyer, Kidnapped,* and *The Scarlet Letter,* she'd have to add these titles to their home reading as well. There were inevitable complaints from Ann and her siblings like, "No one else in my class has to read these books!" but Mom stuck with the plan.

How encouraging it was for Susan to receive Ann's letter in which she expressed her excitement about being exempted from freshman English because she'd already read all the classics and great books assigned for first-year college English and was able to succeed on advanced placement tests.

Mother-Daughter Book Clubs: Building Confidence and Connection

Mother-daughter book clubs have sprung up around the country because reading the same book and talking about it brings you and your girl closer together. Sharing ideas and favorite books you're reading can be an enjoyable bonding experience that has helped many daughters navigate difficult issues in adolescence while staying connected to their moms. She can ask questions she wouldn't feel comfortable discussing in the classroom, and gain different perspectives just from talking with her peers.

Some moms and daughters carry on conversations about what they're reading in spontaneous moments at home or in the car. They also exchange books with each other and share a love of reading.

Other moms want to take a more structured approach to sharing books with their daughters in a weekly or bi-monthly book club. All it takes is to invite another mother and daughter who enjoy reading. Your group can stay small or grow larger, with four to six mom-daughter pairs. Scheduling meetings is easier with a small book group, but those things depend on what you feel would be best. Everyone commits to reading the books and attending meetings for discussion and snacks.

Girls who are nine or ten (or eight if they're more advanced readers) are a good age to start a mother-daughter book club with. You can gather input from your girls as well as their mothers on what books to read. When the daughters have a voice, they'll feel more ownership of the book club. You can get recommendations from the library or local bookstore on titles that are well suited for mom-daughter book clubs. Reading books with strong female characters who are also good role models can be inspiring to our girls. Many books today include discussion questions or guides for book groups, or you can make up your own.

Some mother-daughter book clubs continue from elementary or middle school until the girls graduate from high school; others are for a shorter span of time. You can read the books independently (or read some of the books aloud together at bedtime) and come together with your group to talk about them. While they are enjoyable, mom-daughter book clubs also have many other benefits. Besides improving her reading and comprehension skills, it helps keep the lines of communication open and builds relationships not only between you and your daughter, but with the other girls and moms who join you.

In their new book, *Her Next Chapter: How Mother-Daughter Book Clubs Can Help Girls Navigate Malicious Media, Risky Relationships, Girl Gossip, and So Much More,* Charlotte Kugler and her mother, Lori Day, describe how they formed, structured, and sustained their mother-daughter book club. They offer good advice not only on making the reading experiences and meetings meaningful and fun, but they also discuss issues girls are facing today, like sexism and bullying.[1]

Besides being some of their best times together while Charlotte was in middle school to leaving for college, their mother-daughter book club helped them build not only a literary bond, but an indelible relationship that remains even though Charlotte has grown up.

As they discovered, mom-daughter book clubs can help girls forge strong identities and build their confidence, "inoculating them against some of the more ugly manifestations of pop culture and sexism."[2] But there are other goals of mother-daughter book clubs. It can act as a small village "where women can collectively support girls and model healthy femininity for them . . . a place where they can feel something akin to having sisters, a safe place for girls to express their opinions" and a group where "they feel special about enjoying time spent with their mothers."[3] The book clubs also encourage intellectual curiosity and critical thinking.

In addition, to be reading the same book as your daughter gives you some great common ground to talk about even at other times in the week. While talking about characters in a book, your daughter may open up and discuss something you would have never heard or talked about.

Watching the movie adaptation of a book she's read can be a special time together and stimulate rich discussion. While we're working hard to protect our daughters and sons from dangers, we should make an equal effort to expose them to what is uplifting, noble, and heroic. The website www.teachwithmovies.com is a source of films that offer positive role models and topics for moral discussion. And there are hundreds of good books whose admirable characters will live in a girl's heart and imagination. *Books That Build Character* by William Kilpatrick provides an annotated bibliography of more than three hundred books appropriate for different levels, from early childhood to adolescence.[4]

As you model reading for recreation and also read aloud with your daughter, even after she can read by herself, you're acting as a powerful force in her life as a reader. Reading together is a shared activity that whole families can enjoy, not just girls and moms. It brings bonding and togetherness in a way that few things can.

Writing works the same way. When you write a note to a friend—a lovely thank-you note, not an email or text—or write a letter of sympathy to a friend who's suffered a loss, let your daughter see you. She'll observe that real people write and that writing is not just something teachers assign so students can fill in the blanks on countless worksheets, but that it's really a valuable tool for maintaining relationships.

She'll see that writing, besides being a practical and valuable life skill, can be comforting or encouraging to friends and family. Using everyday opportunities like responding to her questions, reading together, and writing in the course of everyday life makes a real difference because your daughter will tend to emulate you and value the same things you do. What a privilege it is to be a mom with that kind of influence.

When There's a Bump Along the Learning Road

Sometimes things go along well in school for our girls and at times they seem to fall apart. That's when your daughter needs an ally—not a mom who does her work for her or makes excuses for her, but one who helps identify the problem and get the help she needs to get back on the learning road.

Ashley entered a local junior high after having attended a small Christian school since kindergarten. Within the first month, she was quickly overwhelmed with the homework, handing in her work late, and not being able to keep assignments or papers straight. She had been a good student up to this point, but her grades—and motivation—plummeted. Every morning she was anxious about going to school.

Concerned about the changes, her mom looked closer to see what was going on. It wasn't that Ashley didn't want to learn. She realized that disorganization was the main problem. Her mom tried to help her, but their homework sessions led to frustration, so she found a college-aged "study buddy" who helped Ashley organize her notebook and keep track of assignments. Her tutor also shared her secrets for studying for tests and tips for success in the classroom. Ashley listened to her study buddy, and as she got more organized, she began to enjoy her classes more and her grades improved over the semester.

A Mom's Secret to Helping Her Daughter Succeed

Our girls want to be smart and achieve, yet many are stymied in the classroom because they haven't learned to "study smart." Often the issue is that they have different learning styles and needs that are not addressed in the classroom. Scores of moms I've met are bewildered because the bright, curious, happy girl they used to know has shut down to learning, is negative about school, or is underachieving. There are thousands of talented girls who are doing just average or below average at school, and worse, are convinced they aren't very smart because of their lack of success in school.

Early experiences at school can teach our daughter—often for the first time—how she measures up. No matter how much she may accomplish later in life, a "dumb" label that is put on her early on can leave a long-lasting scar.

Why Are Some of Our Girls Not Achieving?

Melissa's baby book had glowing reports of her verbal and social skills. Her mom told me that her little girl had started talking earlier than any of her other children—and hadn't stopped. She had a big vocabulary and could make conversation with anyone she met—and did when they were at the grocery store, on their walks, or at the library. She had a strong bent for music and could remember jingles on television she'd heard only once or twice.

Melissa had some struggles in the early grades but learned to read and got reasonably good grades. She always had a good relationship with her teachers and liked school. However, when Melissa began lagging with her schoolwork in the fourth grade and, on many mornings, said, "I don't want to go to school," her mom grew worried.

So she jumped in to help her with each homework assignment until it was complete. In her great effort to help her daughter, she also told her *how* and *when* to get her work done. The trouble was, mom became a taskmaster, and a power struggle between mother and daughter ensued.

Melissa was trying hard to please her parents and teachers and wanted to make good grades, but all she got were C's or lower. Already pigeonholed as slow in math and science, she spent part of her morning with the resource teacher and other "dumb kids" (as she called her group) who did extra work on math basics. Although she was creative and could write a good story, her self-esteem plummeted.

Her mom began to realize that Melissa was an auditory learner who needed to hear and practice saying information, to be given clear oral explanations rather than being told, "Just read the directions in the book." She had auditory and verbal strengths. But her teacher insisted that students be silent during study time and reread the textbook if they didn't understand rather than letting them ask questions and discuss the difficult parts.

Your daughter may be a verbalizer with auditory strengths like Melissa. She may have an analytical thinking approach that requires things to be presented "in order." She may learn best in a group.

Your girl may be an early-morning learner or one who concentrates and is most alert in the afternoon. Your daughter may be a visual learner or a hands-on, exploratory type of learner.

We can compare the learning style to a television set that can receive information on several different channels. Let's say you're at a lake cabin without cable service or a satellite dish, but there are a few local channels. One channel usually comes in more clearly than the others. And just as you would tend to watch that stronger, clearer channel as the main source of your news and entertainment, each child tends to rely on one means—the auditory, visual, or kinesthetic—as her primary way of *input* (receiving and processing information), and of *output* (expressing knowledge, answering test questions, etc.).

If one station has constant interference and is blocked from effective use and the student doesn't know how to change channels, she can become frustrated and develop problems in the classroom.

But if she knows what her best "channel" or input/processing style is, it will make a big difference. Over and over studies have shown that the students who achieve the most know, perhaps intuitively, what their learning strengths are and how to capitalize on them. At the same time, they will find ways to compensate for their weaknesses so they aren't consistently derailed by them.

While teachers have had in-service seminars on learning and processing styles, few can adapt that information to a whole classroom of twenty-five or more different students. The best person to help identify your daughter's learning strengths and show her how to make the most of it is *you!* I'll give you some starter ideas below that can actually make learning fun. Using them can make a tremendous difference in empowering her to become a more independent learner and help bypass weaknesses as she approaches homework and studies for tests—all throughout her academic career, even into college.

Bringing Out the Best: Helping Our Girls Learn in Style

Movers. Your daughter is active, has a lot of energy, and learns best with a hands-on approach (for example, she figures out how electricity works better with an experiment). She may shine on the athletic field or in dance or gymnastics, but be fidgety when she has to sit for prolonged periods doing pencil-and-paper assignments or worksheets. She's just as smart as any other child and can achieve just as well as other students—if she learns to use her kinesthetic skills:

- Get a whiteboard and have her teach you, siblings, or a classmate the content that needs to be mastered for a test.

- Create a board game with the information that she needs to learn. She can make a spinner, use a large piece of cardboard to make the playing board, add some small playing pieces from around the house, and put the questions on either index cards or directly on the board spaces. Once she gets the hang of this, she'll have great fun creating the board games for study.

- If there are abstract math concepts that haven't "clicked" yet, demonstrate using beans or macaroni to count and other manipulatives from your kitchen. For example, with fractions cut a piece of bread in sections or a pizza in pieces.

- Role-playing, field trips, science experiments, and direct learning experiences will help motivate her to learn in certain subjects.

Lookers. If your daughter has a sharp visual memory, notices small details, likes to complete worksheets, and can memorize spelling words after looking at them for a short time, she may have looker strengths. It's like she has an excellent copy machine in her mind that helps her process and remember visually from the board or a textbook whatever she needs to learn. Here are some examples to help enhance her study:

- Show her how to make an illustrated time line on long butcher paper with history dates and a picture that reminds her of the event. Tape it around her bedroom or playroom.

- Get her started making study cards out of bright-colored index cards to help learn Spanish vocabulary words (English word on front, Spanish on back), math facts, states and capitals, and lots of other information. She can review the cards and put the ones memorized in a different stack until they are all in that group.

- Use three or four highlighters in different colors to categorize parts of speech: green highlighter for nouns, yellow for verbs, blue for adjectives, and pink for adverbs.

Talkers. Does your daughter not only need to see information but to *hear and say* it, perhaps several times, for best understanding and retention? Talkers are very verbal and good at listening and being able to follow oral directions from teachers and parents. Sometimes a teacher thinks she's talking in class, but she may be unconsciously repeating what the teacher said to better understand it. It's like she has a high-quality digital recorder in her brain. She's also usually social, can express her ideas with ease, and likes to work with others in groups. You can maximize her learning by

- encouraging her to turn the information she's going to be tested on into a poem, rhyme, or acrostic.
- having her study with a partner or group. They can discuss the material and together pick questions for a practice test to take and score.
- using a digital recorder or one on your smartphone for her to rehearse the questions and answers she needs to study. She speaks the question into the recorder, waits a few seconds, and goes on to the next question, all the way through the material. Then she presses Play and says the answer after each question. It's a great way to master material.

If your daughter has a combination of these learning styles (which some kids do), she can combine study methods. When our daughter was in school, teaching her the ways she processed information best helped her memorize and learn her school subjects. When I tutored students, these "learning in style" methods often turned around a discouraged or underachieving student.

STEM for Girls

Recently I met a darling college girl named Hannah, an engineering student at the University of Virginia, who was doing an internship at a big aviation corporation during the summer. I asked her how she got interested in a field that young women often don't choose, and she talked about the enthusiasm of a female science teacher in junior high, her chemistry teacher in high school, and a science and engineering camp she attended that broadened her horizons. There she got to do science experiments, create structures out of toothpicks and mini marshmallows, and explore robotics.

STEM stands for science, technology, engineering, and math subjects—career fields that in the past girls weren't encouraged to go into. Plenty of girls have the abilities it takes to pursue these fields, and the career opportunities are wide open.

These subjects aren't just for boys. Here are some signs that your daughter might have aptitude and interest in STEM classes: She likes to solve problems, explore and ask questions about how things work, build or make things. If you have access to science camps and your daughter can attend, she may find she enjoys the hands-on activities and creative opportunities offered. And if you know college girls or women in science or engineering careers, it can be inspiring for your daughter to get to know them.

Another way we can help or support our girls' learning is to introduce them to potential mentors from our local network so they can have real-life experiences in their fields of interests. I like how my friend Carol Hartzog has done this with her daughters. Hannah wants to be a pediatric physical therapist, so she arranged for her to work in the summer at an orthopedic therapy clinic. She also works as a sports trainer with athletic teams at her high school. Her older daughter, Elizabeth, is taking criminal justice courses at a community college half days while taking all her high school courses. She's been able to go on ride-alongs with a policeman in Oklahoma City and participated in an Edmond Police Explorer program, where they learn how to take fingerprints and get to drive a police car. Giving real life experience in the areas our girls are passionate about—whether it's helping at a veterinarian clinic or "shadowing" an attorney on his day at the courthouse—is a great way we can foster their learning and let them see the possibilities ahead.

The sky's the limit when we help our daughters stay curious, become avid readers, overcome learning obstacles, and nurture their unique potential and interests.

Questions to Discuss or Journal

1. What are your learning strengths? What are your daughter's strongest ways of processing information?

2. What ways can you show her to use her learning style to study or memorize more effectively?

3. What is your daughter's center of learning excitement—what she's most interested in learning or pursuing?

4. Discuss or write down specific areas of talent, gifts, skills, and special interests you see developing in your daughter. With a friend, and using ideas from this chapter, talk about how you can encourage these attributes as she grows.

5. What hopes and dreams does your daughter have for the future? How can you nurture these?

13

A Mom Who Helps Develop a Daughter of Character

Kids will care about our values when they know we care about *them*. Emotionally intimate time is especially important for helping our children feel loved and for maximizing our influence on the kind of person they are becoming.

Dr. Thomas Lickona

Recently, I received a letter from our daughter, Alison, and it blessed me so much. Sometimes we truly don't realize the impact our actions have on our children or what values they've internalized. On rare occasions, we get to see a little glimpse of that influence. I've already told you that I've done plenty of things wrong, so perhaps you'll understand why this little window into our daughter's childhood memories and values is a treasure:

Mom, some of my earliest memories as a child had to do with helping other people. What I learned from you and Dad had less to do with what you said than what you did in this arena.

I'd say it was the most impacting and vivid action because somewhere along the timeline it became a part of who I am as well. Not a priority or goal or even a principle, but simply a part of my schema. The way I saw the world as far as being of service and aware of others' needs and personhood came as a direct result of the actions you and Dad took cohesively to be of service to others, to be aware of other people's needs and humanity. You were listeners of stories; you took interest in the lives of others and were looking for ways to help.

But there was also an early detection in my mind and heart that this came from generations before you as well. I felt like I was part of something special and bigger than myself, even as a little girl. I've learned that no matter what, you can always be of service to someone else. This has been a bedrock of my faith in God, a living picture of Jesus reaching out His hands, heart, and "home" to everyone willing to receive help or service.

I remember going to nursing homes with you, visiting older women who didn't have regular visitors. I remember going with you to see Flo, your seventy-plus friend, and seeing how she loved the banana bread you brought and the joy and hospitality she extended in response to our regular visits. Your asking her story, validating her life and existence by consistently engaging in those visits, allowing her to be involved in our family, and showing genuine interest in her life made a big impact on me.

I remember the hours watching, listening, and being a part of these simple and profound visits with the aging ones who often get left behind, are lonely or limited by their physical or circumstantial conditions.

I remember Kathy, the single woman who lived with us for a number of months when I was little, and how natural it felt to invite people who needed a respite to our home . . . with a genuine (not religious or obligatory) love and care for people. I remember the few years Dad had his store, seeing him ready and willing to help anyone who seemed to need it.

Of course the visits to Billie's house are some of the most vivid. The regularity of those, Billie's voice when she'd share thoughts and stories, your listening to her and sharing our life as we grew and things changed. She was an invalid, but I remember her reading to me from her bed in the living room, where she was most of the time. You met time after time after time, and shared your heart in those visits. For years.

I remember how you and Dad valued visits to see your mom, Great Grandpo and Grandmo, Mimi and Pop, above most other things—work, busy-ness, personal gains. You were intentional and consistent, and I saw the effect of that directly in their lives. You taught me how to value the things that are often forgotten in a harried world: the simple kindnesses, the genuine gestures of connecting, sharing family, your time, your food, your finances, your heart.

And even in the tougher times, the tight times, the almost two years in Maine, the moves we made, the years Dad struggled with ongoing depression—you always found people to connect with and share life with and brought me along to experience those times. Like with Louise Montgomery's Friendship House in Portland, Maine, where we brought dinner and mittens for the guests who were homeless, and had come to the Friendship House to live until they could get on their feet.

These times created a fabric woven into my heart, a desire to find ways to help or listen to people's stories and to notice those who are forgotten: the sick, the elderly, the housebound, the hurting, the single mothers, the addicts. The places I didn't see many other parents make time to go. I remember Dad serving at the downtown City Care breakfasts for the homeless and his helping at Ground Zero right after the Murrah Federal Building bombing downtown.

So I'd say that in spite of all the ups and downs, the verbal or nonverbal parenting methods you and Dad implemented, by far the most impacting memories and most influential way you parented have to do with what you DID, who you

ARE, and who you WERE during all those periods of time as I grew up.

Internalizing Values

I've found throughout the years of parenting and teaching students in a variety of ages and classrooms that what Dorothy Law Nolte wrote in a widely circulated poem long ago is just as true today: Children learn what they live.

Through her words, Nolte simply yet profoundly conveyed one of the major ways we pass on character qualities like kindness, fairness, and honesty to the next generation. Two of my favorite lines are:

> If children live with honesty, they learn truthfulness.
>
> If children live with kindness and consideration, they learn respect.

The original version of the poem is quite long, and you can look it up. It's worth pondering because her words are a great reminder of how children learn values and internalize good character.

You see, there is *external* motivation for doing something, but what we want to grow is *intrinsic motivation*—like the internal motivation to do the right thing, to abstain from premarital sex, to study and work hard in school, to be honest and trustworthy. For example, an external incentive for your girl to read more is to reward her with a cupcake every time she reads five books. She might be excited about reading more books for a while—as long as the cupcakes keep coming. Your hope would be that she would at some point "get hooked on books" and read more as a result of sheer enjoyment of books—without the reward of cupcakes. Unfortunately, research does not bear out this approach.

She is far more likely to internalize the value of reading if instead you read with her, go together to the library, and buy her a book on her favorite subject for every birthday rather than be rewarded with treats for reading a certain number of books.

On the flip side, Nolte's poem also includes truths like these:

If children live with criticism, they learn to condemn.
If children live with hostility, they learn to fight.

None of these negatives are the values and attitudes we want our daughters to internalize. So let's look at how we help shape our daughters' character in the fleeting years they are in our homes.

Mama Says

What moral character and values did you learn from your parents? Part of a mother's role throughout the ages has been to shape her children's character and instill values. Parents and the home environment shape their values more than any other influence, especially in the early formative years. In fact, studies show that by the age of five, a great deal of character development has already taken place, and continues to develop throughout the growing-up years.

My mother certainly shaped the values of each of her five daughters and son. So did my father, but he died when we were young. From that point on, Mama was our primary influence. She was not a perfect mom, but she imparted character in a myriad of ways. Mama passed on a strong work ethic by virtue of her role model. She encouraged kindness and forgiveness from the time we were very little, saying it so often it was written on our hearts, especially when we bickered: "Be kind and compassionate to one another, forgiving each other, just as in Christ God forgave you" (Ephesians 4:32). But she also lived those virtues out by her kindness to people in our neighborhood, family, and the world around us in Dallas, Texas.

I still remember Mama's sayings that conveyed important values, like "A penny saved is a penny earned," or "Cleanliness is next to godliness," and boy, did she keep everything in our house clean, even with six children and a busy household.

She taught us that when God closes a door, He opens a window— that when things are difficult, we should keep trying and not give up because things will be better tomorrow. That's a statement of optimism and hope that helped her survive growing up during the Great Depression in a family that suffered horribly and financially because her dad couldn't get a construction job. Mama's hopeful nature helped her thrive, excel in school, and work all through high school to help her family. She also lived through World War II and had friends who died in the war. She was part of the "Greatest Generation" and exuded optimism, inner strength, confidence, and grit in the best of times and the worst of times.

Though it may seem like an old-fashioned word, *grit* is actually a good description of a character trait: it means courage, resolve, and perseverance. The movie *True Grit* was a John Wayne film that featured a fourteen-year-old female character named Mattie Ross who had tremendous determination. The original movie is less violent than the remake of 2010, and it's a good movie to stimulate discussion about courage, grit, and determination.

Mama also imparted the importance of generosity to us by offering delicious meals and warm hospitality to people far and wide. Every Easter when she bought our six pair of shoes to wear Easter Sunday, she bought six children at the Children's Home brand-new shoes as well. That and other generous acts stamped an indelible value of giving to others on my heart and each of my siblings.

A Foundation for Character

So as we've seen, the first place we start building our daughter's character is in our homes. As Dr. Thomas Lickona, developmental psychologist and education professor at the State University of New York at Cortland, said, developing values first "involves treating our children with love and respect, but it goes well beyond that. It has to do with how we treat each other as spouses—something that our children have literally thousands of opportunities to observe.

"Our marital behaviors, we can be sure, will imprint themselves on their moral memories. When we fight, do we fight fair? Do we use disrespectful and denigrating language, or do we maintain in our words and tone a basic respect, even in the heat of an argument? Do we forgive and reconcile soon after, or hold on to our anger and resentment? Healthy families, research shows, commonly have reconciliation rituals that enable them to forgive and make up quickly."[1]

It matters to treat our family members politely, even though we're together on a daily basis. And though husbands and wives sometimes get irritated with each other, your daughter is watching as you say simple words such as *Please*, *Thank you*, and *Forgive me*, and act with civility toward each other. A verse in the New Testament gives us such a good guide for how to treat each other: "Love each other with genuine affection, and take delight in honoring each other" (Romans 12:10 NLT). It's the daily ways we interact in a marriage and family that unknowingly get passed on to our daughters and sons.

Although character curriculum is taught in many schools today with various degrees of effectiveness, as we see, the environment a girl lives in is still her best place to learn ethics and values. And you're the best teacher because you spend the most time with her. Dads have a big responsibility to teach their children solid moral foundations, and we hope they do. Fathers are taking a larger role in their children's lives today, but mothers hold the primary role in their children's character development and can make a lifelong difference.

That's because responsibility, kindness, honesty, cooperation, self-control, determination, and other values influence how our daughters will respond to situations, how they act in the classroom, how they relate to girlfriends, and later, how they will function in their career and relationships. Whether they will keep trying at a difficult task or give up. Whether they will exercise self-control instead of giving in to peer pressure. Whether they will stay committed in marriage or throw in the towel when tough times happen. These are values they learn in the kitchen, at the dinner table, in the car as you drive them to school or ballet class, church, or soccer practice.

A Slippery Slope

Wherever we look in our culture—at the scandals in government, Wall Street, corporate and small-town America, in families and schools—values seem to be deteriorating. That's why, especially today, "If children are to survive and thrive in this society," Lickona said, "it's up to parents to reclaim their authority and instill good values in their children at a very early age."[2]

What our daughters need most is *the value of faith*, he says. Faith in God who created them. A belief system and worldview that will sustain them throughout their lives. Faith is what gives a girl a sense of worth and purpose and helps her get up and move forward no matter what difficulties she faces.

From the cradle through adolescence, the growing-up years are a golden opportunity to instill values in our girls. Character building is a slow, day-by-day process. It's not mastered overnight but by continual modeling, patient instruction, family interaction, and practical application. Yet even if you only get 1 percent growth in your daughter's character each week, you'll see 50 percent growth in a year.[3] Kids are always growing and changing. What they didn't understand today may very well click in six months, or maybe sooner.

What Moms Do

Moms are naturally engaged in the process of character building as we parent, love, wipe tears, feed, nurture, and read books to our children. When we teach our girls to play fair, to not be a mean girl or a bully, and to stand up for those who are bullied, to share, to be responsible for doing their chores, we're building their character. When we teach them by example that *people are more important than things*, that they are to respect others and themselves, we are building a strong foundation for their lives.

As Lynda Hunter Bjorklund said, "Teaching values can naturally lend itself to nurturing relationships. . . . Classrooms for teaching your children values happen at unexpected and unplanned-for times and places."[4]

The World Around Us

We certainly can't depend on the culture around us to impart good character to our children! Newspaper headlines and CNN are filled with the moral failures of people in government and leadership from the top office in Washington to the lowest: CEOs serving time for scams, schemes, and insider trading; policemen who are supposed to be protecting the people but who are sexually abusing women on nighttime traffic stops; professional athletes doping with illegal substances to improve their performances, or hitting their girlfriends and being arrested for assault and battery; priests who abuse children; senators and congressmen in Washington, D.C., who have taken bribes or had affairs and left their families.

Kids are watching all of this, and they are influenced by this moral downslide in our culture and communities. It's one of the reasons there is a crisis of values and cheating is at an all-time high. Students wonder why they shouldn't cheat; they don't even see a reason not to. Bullying has always been around, but the incidences of bullying weaker or younger kids have escalated, even by girls. Lack of respect for sex and epidemic drug and alcohol abuse are characteristics of the lives of many young people who have no moral compass.

You Can Make a Difference

Even with the cultural and moral downslide all around us, you can raise your daughter to become a person of character. It's well worth the effort to be intentional about this part of parenting.

Girls with strong values and character aren't as vulnerable to peer pressure. They develop more confidence and a desire to make a positive difference in the world around them. They are less likely to abuse drugs or alcohol, are more likely to practice abstinence, and are better prepared for the challenges of life. What your daughter learns from you about being honest, thankful, and kind has a powerful and long-lasting influence. Your consistent example can reinforce these values on a daily basis. When you practice, discuss, and read about these values as part of life together, you'll be fostering her growth in morals and character.

What Are *Your* Core Values?

One step in building character is to *decide what core or central values* you want your daughter to learn and live out as she grows. What is most important to you, and what will she need to internalize? A good place to look when you're considering the most important values is the Bible and the teachings of Jesus, like the Sermon on the Mount and passages Paul wrote, like Galatians 5:22. Another helpful place to study values is the book of Proverbs, which is full of descriptions of positive and negative values and the consequences of each.

Learning to Serve

Let's look at a few key values and some ways to develop those, starting with serving others. If you want your daughter to make it a priority to serve others, take her with you so she can see you joyfully serving at a community project. One of the impacting things our granddaughter Caitlin has done is serve meals at the City Rescue Mission downtown with her parents and brother. Through family volunteering nights like this since she was young, she's developing a heart of service. For a number of years, her family has sponsored a child in Africa through Compassion International.

She and her brother and dad came out and volunteered all day at the Outdoor Adventure Day for children of incarcerated parents our nonprofit held this summer. She was a group leader for eight children and had great fun as she took the kids through all the activity stations, played baseball, hula-hooped, and had lunch and great conversations with them.

Mary, a New Jersey mom, took her daughter with her to serve in the Share-a-Meal ministry that started over twenty years ago in their parish. Share-a-Meal was not only to bring a good, healthy meal to those recovering from illness, surgery, or loss of a loved one, but to bring the spiritual food of love, support, and healing to many who hadn't stepped into a church for years, if ever. Many lives were touched and many firsthand examples without words to her daughters happened in the course of serving together over a period of years.

Volunteering gives our girls a deep understanding that they matter, and that while helping someone else, they develop self-worth and find meaning and purpose—even beyond blessing the life of someone else or providing what they need.

Growing in Honesty and Gratitude

If we want our girls to be honest, they need to see us speaking the truth in love—honest and true words—and doing the right thing ethically. Even though it's small, she'll notice when you return the five dollars a cashier mistakenly gave you; she'll see that you don't cut corners. If you want your daughter to not make excuses or not give dishonest reasons, keep that in mind when you want to call in sick at your workplace just because you want the day off or are tired.

Let your daughter see you choosing forgiveness when someone has wronged you. Let her also hear you acknowledge *your* mistakes so she'll know you're human and that we all make mistakes.

When we do blow it and have a bad moment, acting out of anger or rudeness in front of our kids, it makes an enduring impact if we acknowledge it and ask forgiveness of those we were rude to or hurt, including your children.

Growing a Heart of Gratitude

One of the character traits a person needs most in life to experience happiness is gratitude. We can cultivate that value in simple ways at home, like making the writing of thank-you notes part of your family tradition. So many kids don't write thank-you notes when their aunts or grandparents send them a gift.

Gift-giving times are golden opportunities for our girls to practice gratefulness. Every year let her pick out a colorful box of thank-you notes. Then after the holiday, designate a time when the whole family sits down to write notes to each relative who gave them a gift. Even if your little girl is too young to write, have her dictate a short note of thanks for what she received as you write it down. Then she can illustrate the note with a picture—it will mean a lot to the giver. At the same time, you'll be helping her develop two skills: the character quality of gratitude and her writing ability.

As Marcel Proust said, "Let us be grateful to people who make us happy; they are the charming gardeners who make our souls blossom." Have a blessing basket or jar in the middle of the dinner table so everyone can jot down what she is grateful for, and put the notes in the container. Once a week share these at a meal. If you leave a paper trail of gratitude in your life to those who help you or bless you, your daughter will catch the spirit of gratefulness.

This is a small but wonderful thing because gratitude leads to joy. As Brené Brown once said to her children, "I want you to know joy, so together we will practice gratitude."

Hands-On Character Lessons

If you are a homeschool mom, you have a myriad of opportunities to develop your daughters' and sons' values every day. If your children go to a school, you can be creative about providing hands-on character lessons. For example, involving your daughter in planting and growing a garden teaches patience, hard work, and perseverance. If you help her start a collection of small shells or beads and then make jewelry out of them, it develops resourcefulness. You can declare a kindness day, where each member of the family thinks of kind acts to do for others; then come back together at night and discuss them.

Imparting Values Through Stories

One of our favorite ways to impart values to our children was through reading, storytelling, and discussing what we read. When stories take place right alongside your example and hands-on ways to practice them, the values you hold dear and want to pass along to your kids are reinforced in an enjoyable and indelible way.

Stories will give your daughter a sense of who she is and where she came from along with the values your family holds dear, even back a generation or two. Children's books like *The Little Boy Who Cried Wolf* and *Pinocchio* show the importance of being honest and demonstrate the reality of consequences.

Whenever you read aloud classic books like *The Red Badge of Courage* by Stephen Crane, *The Hobbit* by J. R. R. Tolkien, *Charlotte's Web* by E. B. White, *The Black Stallion* by Walter Farley, or *Treasure Island* by Robert Louis Stevenson, you are conveying the importance of courage, hard work, friendship, and patience. *The Chronicles of Narnia* by C. S. Lewis, one of our children's favorite series of all time, has not only a compelling story but priceless and eternal values.

The Dinner Table: A Forum for Values

Family conversation around the dinner table can provide many opportunities for sharing values and beliefs. Besides the fact that many studies show that children who have frequent family meals *achieve more in school* and *are less apt to take drugs and alcohol*, they also learn their family's values and culture around the table.

Start early—begin the family dinner when your children are young so that the pattern will be set. That will make it easier when your kids get older. It can be challenging to find a time with lessons and sports, but family meals are worth making a priority and jugging schedules. No nagging or criticizing at the table. When I taught high school, I saw firsthand that the young people who learned to discuss moral and ethical issues at home were able to agree, disagree, ask questions, and share their opinions much better than other students, and were prepared to tackle difficult decisions they'd face in college and adulthood.

Having positive, interesting people over for dinner is a way to increase the power of your own example. This can be as simple as inviting someone you know who has an inspiring story or who leads an innovative community project. We invited international students who studied at the local university for family dinnertime. They loved to show photos of their family and country and were full of stories.

Another topic of dinner-table talk is people in the news or in your city doing admirable or selfless acts. If you search your local newspaper or online news, there are everyday heroes, stories of integrity, courage, or compassion you can share with your kids. There are also examples of bad character: the latest sports scandal, corruption in high places or local places, violations of human rights. These are also valuable learning opportunities because it shows what not to do.

There is a great storehouse of stories from the Giraffe Heroes Project (www.giraffe.org), which has developed a bank of more than a thousand stories of everyday heroes of all ages who have shown compassion and courage by sticking out their necks for others. People.com also carries stories of ordinary people doing heroic things or helping others under the category "Heroes Among Us." These stories provide countless good role models and inspiration as you share them with your children.

We also need to teach the dangers of pornography, illicit sex, and the value of abstinence. Since we can't isolate our girls and protect them forever—at some point they are going to be out of the nest and on their own—we need to convey and discuss the issues they're going to confront.

As author Marlena Graves suggests, we need to impart a deep knowledge that sex outside its proper context and looking at porn poisons our lives because in those cases, we aren't loving our God, our neighbors, or ourselves.[5] Give your daughter the facts about premature sex, the dangers of rampant sexually transmitted diseases, and oral sex—it is still sex, it is dangerous, and it can be damaging physically and emotionally to the girl. Be the mom and lovingly assert your authority—encouraging abstinence and discouraging sexual activity outside of marriage.

Dr. Meg Meeker, in the findings of the Add Health study of thousands of teens, says that "parents *must communicate* their disapproval of teen sex to their daughters." The study showed that teenagers in grades eight to eleven "who perceive that their mother disapproves of their engaging in sexual intercourse are more likely than their peers to delay sexual activity."[6]

On the other hand, when mothers recommend certain types of birth control, their girls are more likely to take that as approval for premarital sex. Most important, the study's findings showed that whether a girl listens to her parents' advice on these critical issues depends on how connected she is with her mother and father. "Although it is critical that our daughters know the risks involved, a wholesome, ongoing dialogue on the subject of sex and love generally works better than a scary lecture."[7] That goes for discussions about drugs and drinking alcohol as well.

Whether about sex, drugs, alcohol, pornography, or other moral issues, those are important conversations that need to occur between moms and daughters before they are misinformed by their friends. Your voice about these issues—in an age-appropriate way and time—needs to be the one she hears first. If you open the conversation and keep the door open for continued talk on any of her questions, a healthy and ongoing dialogue can develop.

Questions to Discuss or Journal

1. What are the most important core values you want your daughter to internalize and live out in her life? Make a list of them and share with another mom how you plan to help her grow in these areas.

2. What "intangibles" discussed in this chapter do you want to pass on to her, like faith, compassion, gratitude, or values? Which of these are most important to you?

3. Think about a few women you most admire and respect, either alive today or in history. What are the concrete qualities and actions they modeled? Consider sharing these observations with your daughter.

4. What is one activity or long-term project you could do, perhaps that you read in this book, that you would like to begin with your daughter?

5. What is an area of character she needs to grow in? You need to grow in? Brainstorm with a friend how you can give practice with exercising that value.

6. What is your goal for your daughter this year regarding growth in her character? How are you making strides toward that goal?

14

A Mom Who Helps Develop a Healthy Body Image and Femininity in Her Daughter

> Girls of all kinds can be beautiful—from the thin, plus-sized, short, very tall, ebony to porcelain-skinned; the quirky, clumsy, shy, outgoing and all in between. It's not easy though because many people still put beauty into a confining, narrow box. . . . Think outside of the box. . . . Pledge that you will look in the mirror and find the unique beauty in you.
>
> Tyra Banks

Our culture is obsessed with youth, sex, materialism, celebrities, sumptuous food, being beautiful, and having the perfect body. Along with the influences of our culture come countless unhealthy messages about body image that surround our daughters every day. Whether the messages are gained at school or watching TV, online, in movies, or from girlfriends, they have an impact.

There are images abounding that put pressure on girls today to be pretty, not to mention thin, high-achieving, popular, and perfect. Although we can't control or silence all those influences, we *can* help our girls develop a healthy body image by the way we live and think and talk about our bodies. We can lead by example, because the primary way girls develop attitudes about their body is from their mother's role model and messages.

It's especially important that we pass on a healthy body image in the times we live in, where eating disorders are at an all-time high. On any given day, one out of every seven women is struggling with an eating disorder. Thirty-six percent of teenage girls believe they are overweight, and over 50 percent are on diets or obsessed with exercise so they'll have the perfect abs. And although some adolescent boys have body image problems, 90 percent of those with eating disorders are girls.[1]

What can we do to help our daughters not be overwhelmed by the pressure to be thin or the culture of excessive exercise? How can we help them grow up with a sense of the externals that is balanced with all the inside parts that are beautiful?

One of the first places to start is to ask ourselves is, *What do I think about my own body, and where did I get those attitudes?*

The Family Thighs

When I was young, I heard my three big sisters talk about "the family thighs" in a negative light, as in, "Oh my goodness, my thighs are fat just like the other women in the family. . . . No matter how much weight I lose they won't get smaller." I hadn't noticed anything wrong with their thighs because I had only admiration for my lovely older sisters, who were very trim, two of them having won beauty contests. Yet their words carried a weight and power that went in my mind and stuck.

After hearing this self-critical phrase on many occasions, I started looking at my thighs and thinking, *Yep, they're just like the family thighs, too big.* Actually, that was ridiculous, because at the time I was twelve years old, thin, and active, and my thighs were just fine.

It's bad enough when sisters or girlfriends say negative things about their or our bodies, but when body-shaming comments come from our own mothers, it's even more impacting. And unless we become aware of what was transferred to us from our mothers or other women in the family, we tend to pass the shaming on to our daughters.

What attitudes or messages did your mother convey to you in this area? Some women have told me they were nagged by their moms for being too heavy or put on a succession of diets growing up. Their moms counted calories. They were told that every donut or chocolate bar they ate would end up right on their thighs or rear end. One precious gal I know had a mother who criticized everything she wore. (I imagine Mom thought she was helping to refine her daughter's fashion sense.) No matter how carefully she dressed to please her mother, she knew when she came down the stairs, there would be a disapproving word or look.

Does your perception about yourself come from the feedback mirrored to you from peers, family, or society? Is it positive or negative? Whatever body image you have is unconsciously transferred to your daughter, unless you are aware of it and develop a healthier perspective.

"Be aware of what triggers come up for you with your daughters and her size, weight, and looks," Dr. Catherine Hart Weber, psychologist and author of *Flourish: Fully Alive and Growing*, told me. "If you have your own insecurities and issues, deal with them yourself. If you have a negative self-image, negative self-talk, a bad relationship with food, or self rejection, your daughter will pick up on these and you will unknowingly be giving her negative messages through your behavior, attitude and comments."

You may experience triggers of how your mother treated you regarding your body or looks. Or if your daughters are more attractive, you may be jealous and not affirming. If they are sloppy or overweight, you may feel shamed and put them down. If you've suffered with food addiction, you may be fearful that your daughter will struggle with this issue as well.

We can tell our girls, "Honey, you are so pretty, just the right size. You are great just the way you are," when she asks us how she looks before going out the door. But if later she hears us on the phone saying things like, "I hate my muffin top waist. . . . I wish I could lose twenty pounds, and then I'd be happier," then she will likely be on the lookout for parts of her body she dislikes. She may begin to shame herself and not accept the size and shape she is. Instead, if you model self-acceptance, it will go a long way toward helping your daughter accept herself.

Her Primary Voice

When Dr. Weber counsels mothers, she encourages them to reflect a positive sense of self- and body image to their daughters. "It's important to be a safe place for your daughter to be vulnerable, talk openly about these issues, and know she will always be loved and accepted for who she is. Young women will internalize that as their primary 'voice' and feel like that is their belief and their foundation. The primary voice should be from the home. The other voices then are secondary and can be dismissed. They can counteract the negative voices from the positive inner voice from their mother."[2]

Along with that, here are some points for you to consider that help your daughter develop a positive body and self-image:

- Create a safe and healthy relationship with your daughter so she can come home and share without your negative reactions.

- Encourage her to see her value as a woman beyond physical appearance, to see the beauty of her soul, her gifts, and talents.

- Encourage her to be involved in other ways where she is being affirmed, and expose her to positive places where she can feel good about herself (e.g., music, church group, sports, school plays).

- Allow and affirm your daughter's uniqueness. Don't criticize, demean, or be controlling about how you want her to look.

- Affirm her body type and don't expect her to be what she is not—or to fit into certain fashion styles or sizes.

- Encourage her to dress according to her strengths, downplaying weaknesses and making the most of her best features.

- Equip your daughter to discern how to read her own body and soul awareness. This goes for food, influence from the media, social media, and self-image. Help her become more aware of what she needs and the negative influences around her.

It's extremely important to provide supportive relationships and offer companionship and experiences for your daughter. Provide family experiences to attend athletic events and community events.

Healthy Eating

It helps to explore healthy meal options and include your girls in the grocery shopping so they can make healthy choices. Let the little ones push the mini grocery carts and give them several options to pick from so they learn how to make choices on whole grains, fruits and vegetables, and other good foods.

You can invite your daughter into the kitchen from an early age to cook with you and to help her get interested in preparing healthy meals. We can let our girls see that we don't make a big deal out of food but are grateful for our meals, eating healthily, without forbidding all sweets, or bouncing from diet to diet, or trying to put her on one.

Judging Our Girls From the Outside

As mothers, we need to be aware how social media and peer interactions may be negatively influencing our girls. Have open conversations about how she feels about these factors and brainstorm with her on options for change.

Be aware that her self-worth may be based on others' opinions. Many girls fall into this trap. When Kelly was growing up, she was a competitive gymnast. At eleven years old, she moved out of state to live with her gymnastics coach's family in order to train for national and world competitions. She competed from age seven to twenty-one, was a college gymnast, and achieved her dream by making the U.S. Olympic team. Throughout that time, her success and self-worth were based solely on judges' opinions of her performance and appearance.

Knowing the pitfalls, she has been very intentional in helping her seven-year-old daughter develop a bigger perspective. She endeavors to help her see that her sense of self-worth comes from within and isn't dependent on everybody's opinions or external forces. Kelly has an issue with society judging women from the outside, by their appearance, because she knows the toll it took on her life.

One good thing is to have discussions with your girls about where beauty comes from. Where can it be found? A great place to start is how Operation Beautiful describes it: "I can assure you it isn't hidden in the words of any beauty, diet, or fitness magazine article. It doesn't . . . promise a smaller waistline. It's not something that comes out when it is covered up with makeup or ejected from a needle, and it doesn't come included with jewelry or price tags. You won't find it on a treadmill or in the weight room. No—beauty is what lies *within* you. Real, natural, strong, and powerful beauty comes from within your heart."[3]

Looking within the pages of the Bible with your daughter to discover what God says about beauty and the value of a woman can be helpful. As she discovers who she is in Christ, she'll develop confidence and strength in how she is made. Building her character, having fun, helping her discover her dreams, and doing and thinking about what she can contribute to the world instead of how she looks helps her focus on things that matter.

A Girl's Value

In raising her daughter, who is now sixteen, and from counseling many women, Michelle Garrett notices many things moms can do that are vital to helping their girls develop a healthy self-image and lifestyle. First, she often talks with her daughter—and moms in her practice—about the fact that *none of us are defined simply and only by our looks.*

"We are each complex and made up of so many talents, traits, and capabilities. There are things we are passionate about and interested in. We've got to help our daughters know that their value as a person is the sum of all of those parts. Any young girl who thinks her worth is just about her weight or outside appearance is devaluing all the other aspects that make her uniquely who she is."

One issue she discusses with her daughter is about protecting herself by how she dresses, knowing that as girls, we send off the wrong messages to others and to ourselves if we dress in a way that is too revealing or provocative. "I want my daughter to value herself and realize the importance of attracting people who are going to value *her* and not just her body or looks."

Sports are another great way that we can help girls develop an appreciation for their bodies and care for themselves. When girls discover what their bodies are capable of—whether it's running a 10K or winning a swim meet—they start wanting to develop their bodies to reach better performance, not just better looks.

And when girls are part of a team, they experience a great camaraderie and develop relationships. They learn to recognize that each team member plays a different role, but all are distinct and important.[4]

"If as moms we are in the house most of the time, sitting at a computer or watching TV with food within an arm's reach at all times, our daughters will be too," Michelle added. "So get outside with your kids. Find things you can do together that make your hearts sing. You don't even have to be an athlete to enjoy and encourage their activity. Our daughters should be outside running, skating, bicycling, climbing, and swimming."

I made lots of mistakes raising our daughter, but she tells me I did eat moderately ("Moderation in all things" was my family's motto) and was active—jogging, walking, and playing tennis, which I love and still play weekly. When she was young, Alison and I rode bicycles and took walks and hikes, often to a destination like the library or park.

One of our favorite bike destinations in Maine was a little place down the road called Gillespie's that had the yummiest homemade donuts we'd ever tasted. If it was a super cold day (say, temperatures in the single digits), we'd drive after school and enjoy their homemade hot cocoa—with a warm donut, of course—and chat about her day. Not the most healthy after-school snack, but oh, the memories we made at that donut shop.

Cultivating Our Daughters' Femininity

The word *feminine* means characteristic of or pertaining to a woman.[5] Whatever a woman does *is feminine*, because she is a woman. That includes climbing a mountain, riding a motorcycle in leather pants, and entertaining guests in a floral dress.

Femininity is more than being a girly-girl. It means helping your daughter find and celebrate her own style as she grows up—whether that is boho-chic, ruffles and lace, classic Jackie O, or jeans and a T-shirt with boots.

Amanda, a young mother of twins, told me she was a "prissy tomboy," which was a new phrase to me. But it really described Amanda's style of femininity growing up. She often put on one of her princess dresses, choosing either the pink, aqua, or pale purple with sparkles and tulle. She slipped her little feet into matching princess shoes and, with a purse on her arm, went out and made mud pies with the boys under a tree. Or she shed her purse and princess shoes to play football, toss around frogs, or skateboard with the guys.

Janene grew up surrounded by boys. She was the only girl who went fishing with her brothers and the neighborhood boys. But nobody put the worm on her hook. She had mastered that task, even while her cherry-flavored ChapStick was always tucked away in her pocket. In high school she never went out without lipstick and always loved jewelry; she still does. A Secret Service agent and former FBI agent, Janene may have to wear a dark suit and white shirt to work, but her nails are manicured and she's all about being a girl.

Cultivating your daughter's femininity means that when she starts to date, you help her find a balance between letting a man feel masculine and be a gentleman who leads without allowing him to run over her boundaries. Being feminine is about being strong yet knowing that a woman's strength is demonstrated differently than a man's.

I love what Becky Johnson said about the subject: "Femininity is your daughter knowing she is the whole package of beautiful—her body, her brain, her heart, and her soul—and complimenting her in all these areas as you observe wonderful traits starting to blossom. It is teaching her the art of having a good laugh at herself, of seeing the humor in a bad day—to see how it might even morph into a hilarious story if retold from a comic's point of view. It is emphasizing to her over and over that she is God's beloved daughter, above all, and therefore she is never alone, never without love and guidance, even if you are not nearby."[6]

If you talked to ten or twenty people, they'd all have a different opinion about femininity. (I know, because I have.) That's because being feminine takes on different forms and styles. But the important thing is that being feminine is not just external like wearing stiletto heels, but an inside matter of the heart.

And you never know when your little girl is going to emerge as a young woman. When Rachel was born, her mom couldn't get her into a lace dress and bonnet fast enough. But the reality of their life lived in the country surrounded by brothers meant she grew up wearing jeans and overalls more than dresses as a young girl. She'd pull her dark curly hair back in a ponytail and run out the back door to help her younger brother rescue a lost bunny or to make mud pies.

Then one day, near puberty, Rachel went into the bathroom a tomboy and walked out, to her parents' surprise . . . a beautiful young woman. She'd tamed her curls so they framed her face, and added a little pink lip gloss and a dash of mascara. As she walked by in a form-fitting dress, the whole family's jaws dropped with the shock of it. Her dad and brothers immediately grew nervous and protective. But Mom was delighted that her daughter had discovered, in her own way and time, the joy of getting all pretty and feeling like a young woman.[7]

Questions to Discuss or Journal

1. What was your perspective of your body growing up? Did you have any awkward phases you went through or parts of your body you were self-conscious about?

2. What kind of body image did your mom project to you— and what messages did she give you regarding approval or disapproval of how you looked?

3. What are you doing to help your girls not be overwhelmed by the peer or societal pressures to be thin or look perfect?

4. What parts of yourself (weight, midsection, complexion, etc.) have you been self-critical about in your thinking, and on occasion words might have slipped out about these attitudes when your daughter was nearby?

5. What is an idea or two you got from this chapter that you can apply now or in the future to help her grow up with a healthy sense of her body?

6. What are you doing to help your girl develop and maintain a sense of the great value of who she is on the *inside* (rather than what she does or how she looks) and who she is to you and to God? Go on a search together in the Bible to find what God says about the value and beauty of a woman.

15

A Mom Who Nurtures Her Daughter's Potential and Encourages Her to Dream Big

Every great dream begins with a dreamer. Always remember, you have within you the strength, the patience, and the passion to reach for the stars to change the world.

Harriet Tubman

By the time she was eleven, a California girl named Alexandra had already created more than 350 paintings, some selling for $125,000. As you might expect, Alexandra's interest in art started at a young, young age. As a two-year-old, coloring and painting were already her favorite pastimes, and as her love of art developed, she would paint many hours a day. Elizabeth, an eight-year-old girl I met on a trip to Chicago, started Suzuki violin lessons at age three and became a superb violinist with an extensive repertoire by age eleven. The day we talked, she was so excited. She'd just been invited to play at Carnegie Hall.

Elizabeth and Alexandra's experiences illustrate that many talents show up early in life. Each of our girls is unique with an interesting combination of gifts, talents, strengths, and weaknesses. And those who have disabilities or struggle academically are bright and gifted as well. For Leslie, test taking was always difficult, but she worked hard. She went to college and was accepted to law school. Although she graduated in the bottom of her law school class, because of her hard work and great communication and people skills, she beat out the top-of-the-class graduates for a great position as an attorney and became very successful.

Clues and Signs

If we are sharp observers, there are many clues to our daughters' talents. Looking purposefully and tuning in to their style of thinking and doing things can help us discover hidden potential and talent. Even the way their memories work and what they recall can be a sign of potential. For example, musically talented girls often have the natural ability to remember songs, lyrics, and musical patterns; they may also have perfect pitch.

A girl with spatial talent can picture geometric shapes in her mind and see them turned around in relationship with other objects (a visual skill needed by engineers and architects). She tends to think in pictures and remembers visual rather than verbal things. The language-talented girls remember words the best and therefore can memorize a speech with ease, while enjoying debate and reading. Writing poetry or stories comes naturally to these girls, and a literary or journalism career might be a fit for them.

Trust God With Your Dreams

When you understand your daughter's strengths and give her opportunities to develop her talents, there's no telling what she can accomplish—even if she has major challenges to overcome. Take Heather Whitestone McCallum. When she was eighteen months old, a life-threatening infection left her profoundly deaf. In addition to speech therapy, once she began school, her parents had her mainstreamed and encouraged her to use speech at home instead of sign language. Throughout her childhood, Heather loved ballet and worked hard at dance classes, even though she couldn't hear the music. She learned to memorize the counts, then dance to the music God put in her heart.

When she was in the fourth grade, Heather knew she was losing ground academically despite her hard work and study. Even though she knew she would miss her family terribly, she asked her parents to send her to a special school for the deaf in Missouri. There she made up two grades each year and caught up with her classmates. She returned to attend middle school and high school with them and achieved a 3.6 grade point average overall.

In 1995 she became Miss Alabama, and at the national competition, the beauty of her ballet performance—even without the ability to hear the music—left the judges and audiences across the country stunned. Heather became the first deaf Miss America.

What difference did Heather's mother make? Even though teachers said her daughter would never reach beyond a third-grade education or learn to speak, her mother didn't embrace that negative view of her potential. Heather and her mom proved them wrong, and Heather achieved things that looked impossible because of her parents' guidance and constant belief in her.

Heather's third book, *Let God Surprise You: Trust God With Your Dreams*, shares principles she learned at home that helped her achieve her dreams: a positive attitude; believing in a dream; and being willing to work hard, face obstacles, and build a strong support team. Within each book she's written and each message she delivers, she shares that Christ is at the center of her life and faith is her foundation.[1]

Discovering Your Daughter's Talents

As her mom, you know your daughter the best, love her the most, and can spot talent and intelligence that a school or other people often will overlook. All children are born with a lot of potential in one or several areas, and several areas of talent usually work together in concert as they grow up and use them in a career or to impact the world around them. There are four important ways to discover and develop your girl's talents.

First, recognize the different strengths of your daughter even starting at a young age. Observe her as she plays, works, interacts with people, solves problems, and later does homework, and you'll glean insights into how she's wired.

Just as Elizabeth and Alexandra's gifts emerged early, other talents do as well. Musical smarts are seen in girls who don't have to be reminded to practice their instrument or have perfect pitch as a young child. Elizabeth's mom told me she was practically born singing. Once she started violin, she practiced three hours or more a day just because she loved it. "She would pick up the violin on cold winter days and walk around the house playing. It was her second voice," she added.

Young children with strong interpersonal skills are good communicators and seem to understand other people. Lora, a ballet teacher and choreographer I know, told me that from the time she was young, whenever she heard music, she would think flowing shapes and see movements. Kinesthetically gifted people like Lora learn and express themselves best through movement. Young girls who have a passion for drawing, building, and making things often have strength in the area of spatial intelligence or engineering.

The second important principle is to recognize that what seem like negative qualities can be clues of inherent talent or specific intelligence. For example, the argumentative little girl who is constantly asking *why* is showing analytical gifts (even though it may be annoying to you or her teacher). The one who is continually negotiating and debating for her way may have the ability to be an attorney or ambassador when she grows up. And the girl who is called "bossy" on the playground or classroom is actually showing the valuable gift of leadership and administrative gifting. She just needs time and experience to grow into her big personality and leadership potential.

Besides lowering their sense of self-worth, negative labels like *bossy* discourage girls from accepting leadership roles. Being called *bossy* also keeps girls from speaking up, running for class office, or later pursuing politics. Condoleezza Rice, former secretary of state, said, "My parents elected me president of the family when I was four. We actually had an election every year and I always won. I'm an only child, and I could count on my mother's vote." That's a woman of leadership.

Sheryl Sandberg, chief operating officer of Facebook, was called bossy when she was in the ninth grade. Her teacher took Sheryl's best friend aside and said she shouldn't be friends with Sheryl because she was too bossy—right in earshot of Sheryl. Apparently she had a strong spirit, and though the teacher's comments hurt her feelings, she didn't let it hold her back. In adulthood, she is one of the nation's gifted leaders, an author, speaker, and corporate executive who believes the word *bossy* is extremely discouraging to girls.

In fact, along with Girl Scouts of America, Sandberg launched a campaign called "Ban Bossy" to help parents and teachers remove the negative labels they often put on girls who assert themselves or show leadership skills. The campaign is not encouraging meanness, bullying, or aggression, nor is it affirming rude behavior. Instead, as Sandberg said, "Leadership is the expectation that you can use your voice for good. That you can make the world a better place."[2]

When Your Daughter Has a Dream

Victorya Rogers, a Texas mother, talks often with her daughter about her dreams. She encourages her that she can do anything she wants—just not *everything* she wants to do. Her twelve-year-old girl loves to sing, and dreams of being a worship leader. She's gotten involved with the kids' worship team and signed up for training. She is young but sings with a passion. She also loves cheerleading.

"Although cheerleading will most likely not be her lifelong career, we encourage her in that because she's building memories, learning discipline and leadership, and learning how to maintain physical fitness. We often talk of God's plan for our individual lives, and are training both of our kids how to hear the Holy Spirit teach and speak to them as they read the Bible each day," Victorya said.

"Our kids have faced a lot of personal challenges in their young lives, including the death of close family members, and our house burning and having to move. We have always let them know that facing difficult times is God's way of preparing us for the ministry we are to have for others. We remind them there is always good that comes out of every bad time because God is there and He has a plan."[3]

No matter what happens, she and her husband speak life into their children's lives and encourage their dreams.

Throw Like a Girl

Jennie Finch, a champion softball player, encourages girls to dream big and believe in themselves. In her book *Throw Like a Girl*, she shares how sports help girls grow in ways their academic studies won't—in teamwork, in confidence, leadership, and in making the right choices as teenagers. Her story is an inspiring one for girls who are athletically inclined and have dreams to play their sport in college or at professional levels.[4]

The expression "throw like a girl" is what guys say about another guy who pitches or throws the ball badly, so it originally wasn't a compliment. But apparently Mo'ne Davis, the only girl playing in the 2014 Little League World Series, didn't get the negative message.

The thirteen-year-old pitcher of the Taney Dragons, her Philadelphia team that made it to the World Series, got the message: *Throw like a girl*. And did she ever throw! Her fastball pitches flew from the mound at 70 miles an hour and struck out so many boys that the Taney Dragons won a shutout game and beat other teams all the way to the semifinals of the national title—finally losing only to a Chicago team.

Mo'ne, just five feet four inches tall and very lean, has a big heart and talks like a team player instead of a star. Even though she pitched the most watched Little League World Series game ever played, she was humble in talking about it with the press and brought attention to the rest of her team. The girl who is about to start eighth grade will play her favorite sport, basketball, for her school this coming season. She was the *youngest person in history* to ever be featured on the cover of *Sports Illustrated*. Her dream is to someday get a basketball scholarship to attend the University of Connecticut, but along the way, I think she'll inspire many young girls to dream big and work hard in pursuing their sport.[5]

Whether it's on the baseball field, the dance floor, in academics, politics, international relations, or anything else your daughter dreams of doing, it's going to take hard work, perseverance, and dedication to get where she wants to go. "Parents should caution their daughters . . . that real accomplishment takes real effort. I do not know anyone who has got to the top without hard work," said former British prime minister Margaret Thatcher. "That is the recipe. It will not always get you to the top but should get you pretty near."[6]

Dream Big but Stay Grounded

Lucinda Secrest McDowell, author of *Live These Words*, and her daughter Maggie are very much alike in terms of personality. From the moment she was born, Lucinda played music and sang to her baby girl every day. Every night she sang her to sleep. As she was growing up, Maggie absolutely loved music. At age three, she was singing into a wooden spoon as her microphone and using their hearth as a stage. She was born loving to perform. Mom was able to enroll her in dance lessons when she was three. Right before their first recital, all the little girls were so scared. Little Maggie, three and a half by then, looked at them and said, "Mom, I've gone through this entire year of dance lessons just to perform at this recital!"

Her parents saw early on that she had gifts of music and performing and they wanted to encourage those gifts. But though they lived in Connecticut, near New York City, and knew mothers who took their daughters there for modeling and auditions, Lucinda and her husband made a decision early on not to put Maggie forth as a child actress.

"We were purposeful about encouraging her gifts but not pursuing them professionally while she was a child. On the one hand we wanted her to have training in her God-given gifts, but on the other hand we wanted her grounded in her identity in Christ," Lucinda told me, "which for us meant she'd take advantage of opportunities like Christian camp, dance lessons, and being on the dance team in high school."

They sacrificed for Maggie to take voice lessons at the Hartt School of Music and encouraged her in theatre and music, but all on the local level. From age three to eighteen, Maggie was in the church choir, where she learned a lot of classical music. As a child she told them she wanted to be a star. They encouraged her to hone her talents but also to have a balanced life and be well rounded.

"Thinking of a child going into the arts can be interesting for parents; you don't usually dream that for your child," Lucinda said. "Who will really make it? And what is the price of fame? We felt her acting, music, and dancing were God-given gifts. But we wanted her to develop as a person and not just see herself as Maggie the singer."

The four children they have raised range from special education to graduate education, but the McDowells are all about education. By her junior year, Maggie had been in a lot of school and local productions. They knew if she went to college in New York City, she might get a role and never go back to school. They wanted her to attend college and get a four-year degree.

So they told her, "If you really want to pursue a triple major in singing, acting, and dancing, it has to be in another part of the country." Maggie explored colleges and discovered Belmont University in Nashville that had an amazing musical theatre program.

After auditions, admission, and four years of hard work at Belmont, Maggie graduated and went after her dream: to move to New York City and begin auditioning for Broadway productions. She's a professional actor now and has had acting jobs ever since she arrived.

Here are some things this mama learned in guiding her daughter:

- The first important principle is DREAM BIG. Know who your daughter is and who she isn't, and help her discover her unique strengths, weaknesses, insecurities, and gifts. Help her grow her talents, but make sure the priority is developing into a whole person.

- Don't let your focus be to make something happen or pressure your daughter. Let her live her life as a child rather than your living through her.

- Learn her language of love so you can be her encourager. Some of that has to do with being there with her: taking her to auditions and building her up in the midst of rejection.

- If your daughter does make it, she needs to have a solid knowledge of who she is in Christ. "The spiritual foundations are so important; otherwise in rejection she'll be cast down. It's a hard life. You put yourself out there for all your auditions, and the industry is very fickle."

- "It's a minefield out there," as Lucinda says. "But Maggie can handle those pressures because she has a foundation of being a person first, of her faith in God, and knowing this job doesn't define her. She's also a wife and a daughter, a sister and a friend."

- Lucinda and Mike built into Maggie and their other children the importance of being kind and compassionate, and reaching out to help others.

"Go after your dream," Lucinda always told her children. "Whether you apply at this college or graduate school or audition for a play, or go to a foreign country to serve with a mission organization, remember: *Nothing ventured, nothing gained.* What's the worst that could happen? Even if you don't get it, it's okay to take risks and go for it. Nobody ever died of embarrassment."[7]

Whether your daughter wants to be on the women's national softball team, go into the arts, or run for the senate or presidency someday, let it be her dream, not your dreams lived through her. Remember, it's all about her, not about you! It's her turn to pursue her dream, and you can experience the joy of watching and cheering her on the journey.

You have the privilege of guiding your daughter and helping her become a whole person, not just an athlete or entertainer, and being her encourager while loving her unconditionally along the way. The sky is the limit for girls today! When girls headed to college several decades ago, advisors recommended they become nurses, teachers (still great fields), or secretaries. Today they are encouraged to become business leaders, senators and governors, psychologists and professors, astronauts, paleontologists, chemical engineers, producers and directors, graphic designers, and landscape architects. A world of opportunity is open to them.

Questions to Discuss or Journal

1. What is your dream for your life and the purpose you believe God has for *you*, both now and in the future, when your children grow up?

2. What areas of talent or gifting have you seen in your daughter?

3. What are clues that you've seen of these gifts?

4. Is there a trait that appears negative now but may actually be a sign of her potential?

5. What is your daughter's dream to do or be when she grows up, or an area of the arts, dance, sports, music, technology, business, or *any other interest* that she wants to pursue and is passionate about?

6. What training does she need or opportunities to hone her skills? What may be her biggest obstacle toward reaching her dream?

Living, Launching,
and Letting Go

Perhaps parents would enjoy their children more if
they stopped to realize that the film of childhood can
never be run through for a second showing.

Evelyn Nown

Have you ever responded "Later!" to your daughter's attempt to
show you a spotted green lizard she found on the sidewalk or a giant
white cloud that looks just like a dragon? Perhaps on your way to
adulthood and motherhood your sense of wonder and awe faded
and was replaced by practicality or work, worries, and busyness.

Mine did. With the addition of each of our children, my schedule
got more hectic. I supervised school activities, sports, and homework. I juggled writing deadlines, volunteered at church, and helped
in my husband's business.

"Mom, why don't you go outside with us and have some fun?" I
remember Ali asking me several times on a particularly hectic week.

As I thought about it, I began to see I was missing a lot of outdoor fun and the small miracles God placed along my path. I wanted to share in their joy and sense of discovery—*but there is so much to do*, I thought.

Finally, quite frustrated, I asked God, "What can I do to get off the treadmill?"

Quietly, His Spirit seemed to whisper, "Go fly a kite!"

"Oh, Lord," I replied. "That seems so silly and impractical."

"That's the point," He responded.

So I went to the toy store and bought a kite to fly at our next outing to the park. It had rained that morning but was starting to clear off. Chris and Justin enjoyed the challenge of getting the kite up to catch the breeze, and Alison most of all loved having her turn to fly it. But eventually all three got interested in doing other things. As they ran off to play, I was left holding the string.

As the bright red-and-blue kite swept up and flew almost out of sight, my spirits soared. The breeze blew my hair, and a fresh sense of wonder blew over my heart. I forgot all the things I needed to accomplish and reveled in the blue sky, the huge cascade of clouds. Then, as I gazed up, there it was! A spectacular double rainbow! A double promise, a double blessing.

Flying the kite not only refreshed my spirit and was a great time with my children, but it pointed me upward, toward God, who knew what would make my heart sing. Not just that day, but on many days and even years.

Power Struggles

As mothers, we are trying to prepare our girls for what's ahead, hoping they'll listen to and accept at least some of our advice. All the while they're trying to spread their wings. So what can we do when a tug-of-war or mother-daughter conflict erupts? For me, the first step toward a better relationship with my Alison was on my knees.

At a certain point when our relationship grew strained, when Ali was about fifteen, I asked God to reveal some "majors" I needed to focus on: the need for me to listen better and accept our differences, and to stop being frustrated about or exerting control in areas He pointed out were "minors." Like her hair.

It's amazing how a little thing can cause big conflict. But Alison's hair had become a power struggle. Ever my creative girl, she wanted to cut it short and dye it burgundy. I envisioned a horrid red hue spoiling her lovely, naturally blond shoulder-length hair. Since I was paying for beauty-shop expenses, I thought I ought to have a little input. She disagreed. Conflict grew over the hair issue. Frustrated, I asked, "Lord, what do you want me to do? You know what she'll look like with those wild colors."

"Release her," He said. Not exactly what I'd hoped to hear.

Yet one day soon after, when Alison was in the kitchen, I said, "Ali, your hair is yours to do with whatever you want. Your room is too (the second biggest source of tension)—we'd prefer you keep it clean, but no more nagging or going in and picking up."

With a smile, she agreed. While I wasn't thrilled with her sometimes-messy room or all the creative hairdos and colors she paraded to the breakfast table each morning, transferring responsibility to her provided one less opportunity for conflict. Someone once said that the pulling away of adolescents from their mom and dad is divinely inspired. With relief, I realized Alison's attempts to be more independent were entirely normal and in fact, right on schedule. It meant I needed to let go in some areas—and entrust her to her heavenly Father.

Ironically, besides earning a degree in psychology and being a mother, Alison also is a terrific barber. Now she's cutting my hair and many other people's.

Be encouraged that it's not ever too late to go to your daughter and work toward a better relationship. Because we're all imperfect mothers, most of us haven't lived up to our daughters' expectations, even with our best efforts. Once they reach adolescence or early adulthood, many daughters feel their moms have disappointed or hurt them at some point, and some of those criticisms are based in the reality of our mistakes. When we realize that something we did in the past has hurt her heart or harmed her life, it can have enormous healing benefits on the relationship to admit it to her. Two simple words—*I'm sorry*—if sincerely spoken, can bridge the wide gap between mom and daughter and lead to reconciliation.[1]

The Seasons of Our Lives

Maybe your home is still filled with the sounds and steps of little or big children that run and jump and exuberantly laugh at the smallest things. A friend told me once, "In two years my daughter will be off at college! I wish I could make everything slow down; it's moving way too fast."

We can't make time stop as our children grow, but we can live wholeheartedly while they are with us, and continue to live wholeheartedly when they have launched.

First, it helps to see your life in seasons. Remember that our lives change and no situation your family is in will stay the same. Five or ten years down the road, our lives and possibilities will be different. Recognizing this is important, because we have a tendency to think we have to do everything this year or achieve certain goals by age thirty or thirty-five.

I sat next to a woman on a plane not long ago who had raised five children. After they left the house, she earned a master's degree in criminal justice and worked with young people who were in trouble with the law. Then she went on to earn another master's degree in psychology. When I met her, she had practiced as a marriage and family counselor for over ten years and was more energetic than most thirty-year-olds. This inspiring mother and grandmother was pursuing goals and dreams she wanted to fulfill—and still going strong in her sixties.

As Dr. Hunter says, there is world enough and enough time to dream new dreams, pursue new careers, and focus energies in different directions after your children are raised. "We can have it all—but not all at once. And if we live each day fully, we won't look back over the terrain of our lives with emotional pain because we were inaccessible to our families while our children were at home."[2]

Looking to God

Let me encourage you, as you finish this book, to take all your daughter's needs and all your burdens to God. Ask Him how to apply the things you've learned in this book. Scan through the chapters and consider what your daughter's most pressing needs are right now. And then ask for His wisdom and respond in these areas. He can equip you in every way to be the mom you want to be for her, not only in this stage but also all the ones to come.

Look at your capability and your capacity. Surely you are capable of many, many things: being a PTA president, taking on the challenges of your full- or part-time career, being homeroom mom, teaching and leading, and everything else. Being involved, vital, and energetic are good things. So is commitment.

Be wise, though. As physician Richard Swenson says, "Chronic activity overload is a toxic condition."[3] Doing "everything" can bring stress to our relationships and disconnection with the ones we love the most. In addition, chronic busyness is a recipe for burnout, overload, and exhaustion that causes us to lack the energy we need for life—both for mothers at home and those who are the primary breadwinner or have a demanding job.

Moms who are working and parenting often feel guilty they're not at home or with their kids enough, and at the same time feel bad that they're not achieving as much as they can in their career. They're up until midnight baking cookies for a school function and rushing to get one child to the doctor, another to Tae Kwon Do. Give yourself grace, Mom. Remember, there is no perfect mother. Trying to be the perfect mom sets us up for failure and frustration because we're all imperfect women in an imperfect world with wonderful but imperfect children.

Too often we wrestle with packed schedules; it's been this way for families for decades. Sixty years ago the wife of aviator Charles

Lindbergh, Anne Morrow Lindbergh, wrote, "There is so little empty space. The space is scribbled on, the time has been filled. Too many activities, and people, and things. . . . For it is not merely the trivial which clutters our lives, but the important as well."[4] How can we discern what things are cluttering our lives or making us too busy?

If you ever feel like you're in overload or too many things have cluttered your life, find a way to unplug for a few moments or hours and consider what, if anything, needs to change, what you could say no to in order to say yes to other things.

Your slow-down window of time may not involve flying a kite as I did, but instead spending quiet moments over coffee before the family is awake, lying on a quilt with your daughter, looking up at the night sky's constellations, or sitting on the edge of her bed to listen and pray for her concerns. Taking time for a walk, sharing an ice-cream sundae, or snuggling in sleeping bags while you read by the fire may be the mothering moments that will refuel you.

As one writer has observed, "We've become a nation that feels enormous pressure to drag our children from activity to activity and to cram as many things onto our calendar as possible. It's become an American value or status symbol to overschedule yourself and your kids."[5] You can avoid letting your kids get so busy and overcommitted that you're rushing in different directions with too much to do and not enough time to do it. One thing that helps is to let each child pick one extracurricular activity per semester and decide on at least one activity to do together as a family each week. Then next season they choose the activity or sport they want to do. That leaves time to stay connected and nurture the relationships with your children and those you hold dear.

Even in the midst of your active parenting years, you can be developing your gifts and talents, be involved in your homeschool co-op, and encourage other mothers around you. If you love painting, set up a corner of a room to paint. If gardening is your passion, let the yard be your canvas. If you love writing, schedule small blocks of time to pursue your craft.

In everything, walk in gratitude and ask for the empowering of the Holy Spirit, because God can and will multiply your time. Someone once said, "God can do in twenty minutes what it takes us twenty years to do."

And remember, life is a gift—even if it's a messy life with sticky fingerprints on your wall, unsolved problems, and ongoing struggles. Every day with your children, your family, and your loved ones is a gift. As you give yourself and your time to God daily, keep in mind what really matters, what's most important. Then, like the girl who spun straw into gold in the fairy tale, you can use this time and see the moments and memories turn into gold.

Questions to Discuss or Journal

1. Ask God how much capacity He wants you to use, because it's different from your capability.

2. What can you do to enjoy and savor the time you have with your daughter? How are you making the most of those fleeting years of mothering?

3. What moments have you had where you sensed the fast pace of time and the leaps of growth in your kids?

4. What has God designed you for and *for you* in this season of your life?

5. What really matters to you and your family? Are you using your time to do these things?

6. What are a few ways you could make some margin for some slow-down spots of time? What are your favorite ways to do this?

Acknowledgments

I first want to express many grateful, heartfelt thanks to my husband, Holmes, who has stood by me while writing this book and many others over the years: for neck rubs when it's hurting from hours at the laptop, for Starbucks lattes you've surprised me with, for encouraging words and patience, and much more. I love you!

Thank you dear Ali for sweet notes, meals you've made, and being the best daughter I could ever ask for—plus the wisdom and experience you shared with me about growing up with me as your mom. Thanks for the grace you've extended.

A sincere thank-you to the Bethany House Publishers team, including my editors Jeff Braun and Tim Peterson, the marketing and publicity folks, and all who contributed to this book becoming a reality and getting into the hands of readers. I love working with you all.

To my best-ever favorite agent, Greg Johnson, president of WordServe Literary Group. Thank you for being my creative collaborator, partner in ministry, and wise advisor.

Connie Willems, I can't thank you enough for that day at Panera when we talked (and talked) and you shared some pivotal insights that helped me gain the focus and perspective I needed to continue writing this book.

Thanks to the many mothers who shared their stories and insights about raising girls: Tiffany Fuller, Maggie Fuller, Debb Hackett, Lindsey O'Conner, Kelly Funderburk, Wynne Terlizzi, Anne Marie Miller, Becky Johnson, Lucinda Secrest McDowell, Ashley Morris, Stephanie Thompson, Katie Moore, Shauna Austin, Carol Hartzog, Patti West, Carolyn Helker, and many others—you know who you are. A shout-out of thanks to five awesome young women: my granddaughters Caitlin, Josephine, and Lucy, and great-nieces Madison and Elona—wonderful girls who bring me much joy.

For prayers and encouragement, I am so thankful to Susan Stewart, Janet Page, Peggy Stewart, Jennifer Kennedy Dean, Glenna Miller, Jill Miller, Carolyn Curtis, Corrie Sargeant, Pat Fuller, Cynthia Morris, Betsy West, and my family and friends. May you be blessed beyond what you could ask for or imagine.

To the professional counselors, psychologists, journalists, educators, and child development specialists—Michelle Garrett, Brenda Hunter, Kristen Blair, Leslie Vernick, Pamela Toohey, and Catherine Hart Weber—special thanks for your wisdom, advice, and personal stories. And my sincere thanks to Thomas Lickona for his help and his contributions to the field of childhood education and character development in children.

Notes

Chapter 2: A Mom Who Bonds and Connects With Her Daughter

1. Christie Mudie, "7 Brilliant Ways to Bond With Your Bump," *Mother and Baby*, http://www.motherandbaby.co.uk/2014/04/7-brilliant-ways-to-bond-with-your-bump.

2. Katherine Harmon, "How Important Is Physical Contact With Your Infant?" *Scientific American*, May 6, 2010, http://www.scientificamerican.com/article/infant-touch/.

3. Ibid.

4. Heartfelt thanks to counselor and mother Michelle Garrett for her insights on interruptions to attachment.

5. My grateful thanks to Katie Moore and Shauna Austin for their honesty and transparency. You were kind enough to dialogue with me about your mothering experiences, and I thank you!

6. Cathie Kryczka, "Bonding With Your Baby," *Today's Parent*, August 23, 2004, http://www.todaysparent.com/pregnancy/newborn-care/bonding-with-your-baby/.

7. Jaylene Mory, nurse midwife, quoted by Kryczka, "Bonding With Your Baby."

8. Ibid.

9. My deep appreciation to Dr. Brenda Hunter, author of *The Power of Mother Love,* as well as *From Santa to Sexting* and other books, for sharing her thoughts and research with me, and also for being a constant champion for babies.

10. See more of Dr. Brenda Hunter's wisdom on raising children in her book *The Power of Mother Love*. It's one of the best books I've ever read about the transformative connection between mother and baby and research-based ways to strengthen the bond.

11. Gary Chapman and Ross Campbell, *The 5 Love Languages of Children* (Chicago: Northfield Publishing, 2012), 17.

12. Ruth Nemzoff, *Don't Bite Your Tongue: How to Foster Rewarding Relationships With Your Adult Children* (New York: Macmillan, 2008), 167.

Chapter 3: A Mom Who Listens With Her Heart

1. Steven W. Vannoy, *The Greatest Gifts I Give My Children* (New York: Simon and Schuster, 1994), 110.

2. Thomas Lickona, *Character Matters* (New York: Touchstone, 2004), 39.

3. Ann Caron, *Mothers to Daughters: Searching for New Connections* (New York: Henry Holt and Company, 1998), 14–15.

Chapter 4: A Mom Who Is Present and Engaged

1. Pew Research Center statistics on http://www.pewresearch.org/fact-tank/2013/09/12/its-a-womans-social-media-world/.

2. Results of a survey of five hundred respondents from March 27 to April 9, 2014 reported in *More*, published by the Meredith Corporation, Des Moines, Iowa, July/August 2014, 57.

3. Catherine Hart Weber, *Flourish: Fully Alive and Growing*. This is a terrific book that helps us see whether we are just surviving, and if so, how to begin thriving and flourishing. For more information on her book, visit www.howtoflourish.com.

4. Sylvia Hart Frejd and Archibald Hart, *The Digital Invasion: How Technology Is Shaping You and Your Relationships* (Grand Rapids, MI: Baker Books, 2013).

5. Johann Wolfgang von Goethe, pubic domain.

6. Gary Chapman and Ross Campbell, *The 5 Love Languages of Children* (Chicago: Northfield Publishing, 2012).

7. Julie Jensen, *The Essence of a Mother: Being Conscious of the Sacred Moments of Motherhood* (Guilford, CT: Globe Pequot Press, 2014), 20.

Chapter 5: A Mom Who Helps Her Daughter Navigate the Digital World

1. Brenda Hunter and Kristen Blair, *From Santa to Sexting: Helping Your Child Safely Navigate Middle School and Shape the Choices That Last a Lifetime* (Abilene, TX: Leafwood Publishers, 2012).

2. My thanks and great appreciation to Kristen Blair for the advice she shared with me via phone interview on navigating the digital world of our children.

3. Quoted from *The Wall Street Journal* in The Week, March 28, 2014, 18.

4. Claire McCarthy, "Texting and Teens: A Pediatrician (and Mom) Speaks Out," http://healthyliving.msn.com/pregnancy-parenting/kids -health/texting-and-teens—a-pediatrician-and-mom-speaks-out-1.

5. Barbara Ortutay, "FTC Officials Say Snapchat Deceived Its Customers," *The Oklahoman,* Business: Nation/World, Friday, May 9, 2014, 3C.

6. Kristin Peaks, "7 Dangerous Apps That Parents Need to Know About," *Checkup Daily,* Cook County Children's Hospital, Ft. Worth, Texas, April 16, 2014, http://www.checkupnewsroom.com/7-dangerous -apps-that-parents-need-to-know-about.

7. Gabrielle Donnelly, "Julianne Moore Reveals Why She 'Stalks' Her Children on Facebook," *Daily Mail,* February 15, 2014, http://www .dailymail.co.uk/tvshowbiz/article-2560418/In-opinion-dont-privacy -youre-16-Julianne-Moore-reveals-stalks-children-Facebook.html.

Chapter 6: A Mom Who Encourages and Builds Confidence

1. Quoted originally in my book *The Fragrance of Kindness: Giving the Gift of Encouragement* (Nashville: Thomas Nelson, 2000), 24.

2. For more information, visit www.LanaIsrael.com.

3. Dr. Dweck, now professor of psychology at Stanford University, is a specialist in the field of motivation and education, and has conducted studies like this for over ten years, contributing much to our understanding of how children perceive themselves as learners.

4. With sincere thanks to Dr. Catherine Hart Weber, author of *Flourish: Fully Alive and Growing,* 2013. Visit www.howtoflourish.com.

5. Anne Ortlund, quoted in *The Fragrance of Kindness: Giving the Gift of Encouragement,* 17.

6. Reb Bradley, quoted by Adrian Warnock, "Eight Ways Parents Can Make Sure They're Not Controlling or Overprotective," September 15, 2011, http://www.patheos.com/blogs/adrianwarnock/2011/09/eight-ways

-parents-can-make-sure-they-are-not-too-controlling-and-over-protective/. Bradley's original essay appeared at http://www.familyministries.com /HS_Crisis.htm.

7. Jonel Allecia, "Helping or Hovering? When 'Helicopter Parenting' Backfires," NBCnews.com, May 26, 2013, www.nbcnews.com/health /kids-health/helping-or-hovering-when-helicopter-parenting-backfires -f6C10079904.

Chapter 7: A Mom Who Helps Her Daughter Learn to Manage Emotions

1. Justin, Chris, and Alison, I am so sorry for my lacks in that area and ask your forgiveness.

2. Cathie Kryczka contributes regularly to *Today's Parent*.

3. Many thanks to Pamela Toohey, Coordinator of Child Trauma and Resilience, Oklahoma Department of Mental Health and Substance Abuse Services, for her wise advice and insights on teens' stress and helping them manage their emotions and develop resilience and coping mechanisms.

Chapter 8: A Mom Who Understands Her Daughter's Personality and Encourages Individuality

1. Cheri Fuller and Ali Plum, *Mother-Daughter Duet: Getting to the Relationship You Want With Your Adult Daughter* (Colorado Springs: Waterbrook Multnomah, 2010).

2. Harriet Beecher Stowe, *The Pearl of Orr's Island* (Carlisle, MA: Applewood Books, 2010 edition), 202.

3. Based on an interview with Dr. Chess before her death; Stella Chess and Alexander Thomas, *Know Your Child: An Authoritative Guide for Today's Parents* (New York: Jason Aronson Inc., 1994).

4. Tanya Altmann, quoted by Laura Flynn McCarthy, "Parenting by Personality," *Working Mother*, June/July 2010, http://www.workingmother .com/2010/5/home/parenting-personality.

5. Becky Johnson and her daughter Rachel Randolph coauthored *We Laugh, We Cry, We Cook* (Grand Rapids, MI: Zondervan, 2013) and *Nourished: A Search for Health, Happiness and a Full Night's Sleep* (Grand Rapids, MI: Zondervan, 2015).

6. Mel Levine, *A Mind at a Time* (New York: Simon and Schuster, 2002), 46.

Chapter 9: A Mom Who Prays for Her Daughter

1. Tina Fey, *Bossypants* (New York: Little Brown and Company, 2011), 261–262.

2. My friend Fern Nichols wrote a book on the subject of moms and prayer: *Every Child Needs a Praying Mom* (Grand Rapids, MI: Zondervan, 2003).

3. Ole Hallesby, *Prayer* (Minneapolis: Augsburg Books, 1994 edition), 18–19.

4. Hallesby, 18.

5. A brief summary of Florence Chadwick's life is found at http://www.queenofthechannel.com/florence-chadwick.

6. E. M. *Bounds on Prayer* (Peabody, MA: Hendrickson Publishers, 2006 edition), 172.

7. Statistic obtained from Census.gov, 2010.

Chapter 10: A Mom Who Nurtures Her Daughter's Faith

1. A description I use in my book *Opening Your Child's Nine Learning Windows* (Grand Rapids, MI: Zondervan Publishers, 2001).

2. William Wordsworth, 1770–1850, "Ode: Intimations of Immortality From Recollections of Early Childhood," www.bartleby.com/101/536.html.

3. John Drescher, *Seven Things Children Need* (Scottdale, PA: Herald Press, 1976), 129.

4. Robert Coles, *The Spiritual Life of Children* (Boston: Houghton Mifflin, 1990), 308.

5. Cheri Fuller, *Opening Your Child's Spiritual Windows* (Grand Rapids, MI: Zondervan Publishers, 2001).

6. For more information, visit www.4to14window.com, a global missions movement.

7. Lucinda Secrest McDowell shares her wisdom in her most recent book, *Live These Words: An Active Response to God* (Kingwood, TX: Bold Vision Books, 2014). Visit http://lucindamcdowell.wordpress.com.

8. Leslie Vernick, counselor and life coach, quoted in *Mother-Daughter Duet: Getting to the Relationship You Want With Your Adult Daughter.*

9. Quoted by Kate Shellnutt, "33 Under 33. Thought That Millennials Are Leaving the Faith? They're Actually Leading It," *Christianity Today,* July/August 2014, 35.

10. Shellnutt, 41, 43.

11. Jeremiah 29:11.

12. Tom Lickona, "Do Parents Make a Difference in Children's Character Development?" November 20, 1998, https://www2.cortland.edu/dot Asset/4e26603a-86bb-4c2a-b111-d590dc4e1dce.pdf. Used by permission of author.

13. Jim Burns, "Pass a Legacy of Faith on to Your Kids," April 24, 2014, *HomeWord*, http://homeword.com/articles/pass-a-legacy-of-faith -to-your-kids/#.VFp_YVM1BO8.

Chapter 11: A Mom Who Is a Good Role Model

1. "There Are Little Eyes Upon You," by Edgar Guest, 1881–1959. Although the author of this poem is often thought to be unknown or anonymous, poet Edgar Guest, a prolific British-American author of hundreds of poems about children and family, actually penned it. The poem has appeared in different forms down through the years; I have taken the poetic license to adapt it for mothers and daughters.

2. Steven W. Vannoy, *The 10 Greatest Gifts I Give My Children* (New York: Simon and Schuster, 1994),196.

3. Grateful thanks to Michelle Garrett, licensed professional counselor, for her insights on role-modeling a healthy body image.

4. Brené Brown, *The Gifts of Imperfection* (Center City, MN: Hazelden, 2010), 61.

5. Elayne Bennett, *Daughters in Danger: Helping Our Girls Thrive in Today's Culture* (Nashville: Thomas Nelson, 2014).

6. Ibid., 97.

7. Ibid., 98.

8. As quoted by Cynthia Dailard, "Recent Findings from the 'Add Health' Survey: Teens and Sexual Activity," *The Guttmacher Report on Public Policy*, August 2001, http://www.guttmacher.org/pubs/tgr/04/4/ gr040401.html.

9. Thanks to Caitlin Fuller for her candid comments about growing up.

Chapter 12: A Mom Who Fosters Her Daughter's Learning

1. Lori Day and Charlotte Kugler, *Her Next Chapter: How Mother-Daughter Book Clubs Can Help Girls Navigate Malicious Media, Risky Relationships, Girl Gossip, and So Much More* (Chicago: Chicago Review Press, 2014).

2. Steve Pfarrer, "How Mom-Daughter Book Clubs Can Help Girls," Mount Holyoke College News and Media, May 29, 2014, https://www.mtholyoke.edu/media/how-mom-daughter-book-clubs-can-help-girls.

3. Lori Day and Charlotte Kugler, *Her Next Chapter*, 4–5. See www.motherdaughterbookclubs.com for resources, recommended books, and more.

4. William Kilpatrick, *Books That Build Character* (New York: Touchstone, 1994).

Chapter 13: A Mom Who Helps Develop a Daughter of Character

1. Thomas Lickona, quoted by David Streight, *Parenting for Character: Five Experts, Five Practices* (Portland, OR: Center for Spiritual and Ethical Education, 2008). Used by permission of the author.

2. Thomas Lickona, quoted in "Raising a Moral Child," *Child* Magazine, December/January 1993), 130.

3. Dr. Flip Flippen, family and adolescent counselor, Bryan, Texas, quoted from a personal interview.

4. Lynda Hunter Bjorklund, quoted by David and Jan Stoop, eds., *The Complete Parenting Book* (Grand Rapids, MI: Revell, 2004), 257, 259.

5. Marlena Graves, "Raising Christian Kids in a Sex-Filled Culture," *Christianity Today*, November, 2013, www.christianitytoday.com/women/2013/november/raising-christian-kids-in-sex-filled-culture.html.

6. Dr. Meg Meeker, quoted in Elayne Bennett, *Daughters in Danger*, 110.

7. Ibid.

Chapter 14: A Mom Who Helps Develop a Healthy Body Image and Femininity in Her Daughter

1. "Understanding Eating Disorders in Teens," WebMD, March 17, 2013, http://teens.webmd.com/understanding-eating-disorders-teens.

2. From a personal interview with Dr. Catherine Hart Weber.

3. "What Is Beauty?" http://www.operationbeautiful.com/what-is-beauty/.

4. My thanks and appreciation to therapist and mother Michelle Garrett, Edmond, Oklahoma, for her insights on raising girls to have a healthy body image and lifestyle.

5. *Webster's Seventh New Collegiate Dictionary* (Springfield, MA: G. & C. Merriam Company, 1965), 307.

6. Becky Johnson and daughter Rachel Randolph are coauthors of *We Laugh, We Cry, We Cook: A Mother and Daughter Dish About the Food That Delights Them and the Love That Bonds Them* (Grand Rapids, MI: Zondervan Publishers, 2013). Their newest book is *Nourished: A Search for Health, Happiness, and a Full Night's Sleep.*

7. Becky Johnson and Rachel Randolph, *We Laugh, We Cry, We Cook.*

Chapter 15: A Mom Who Nurtures Her Daughter's Potential and Encourages Her to Dream Big

1. Heather Whitestone McCallum, married with three boys, received a cochlear implant to be able to hear and respond to her son's cries for help. She has been a courageous advocate for disabled and deaf people and served on presidential councils. Her STARS program emphasizes the five keys learned from her parents that led her to overcome her disabilities and achieve her dreams.

2. Cynthia McFadden, "Sheryl Sandberg Launches 'Ban Bossy' Campaign to Empower Girls to Lead," *Good Morning America*, March 10, 2014, http://abcnews.go.com/US/sheryl-sandberg-launches-ban-bossy-campaign-empower-girls/story?id=22819181.

3. Victorya Rogers, life and relationship coach and former Hollywood agent, is the author of several books, including *How to Talk About Jesus (Without Freaking Out)* and *The Day I Met God.*

4. Jennie Finch, *Throw Like a Girl: How to Dream Big and Believe in Yourself* (Chicago, IL: Triumph Books, Random House, Inc.), 2011.

5. Scooby Axson, "Mo'ne Davis on This Week's National *Sports Illustrated* Cover," August 19, 2014, *Sports Illustrated*, http://www.si.com/more-sports/2014/08/19/mone-davis-little-league-world-series-sports-illustrated-cover.

6. Quoted in Elayne Bennett, *Daughters in Danger*, 107.

7. My thanks to Lucinda Secrest McDowell for sharing her and Maggie's story about how she dreamed big and pursued that dream. Lucinda's books include *The Role of a Lifetime*, *Quilts From Heaven*, and her most recent, *Live These Words: An Active Response to God* (Kingwood, TX: Bold Vision Books, 2014), www.encouragingwords.net.

Epilogue: Living, Launching, and Letting Go

1. Adapted from Cheri Fuller and Ali Plum, *Mother-Daughter Duet: Getting to the Relationship You Want With Your Adult Daughter* (Colorado Springs, CO: Multnomah Waterbrook, 2010), 192.

2. Brenda Hunter, *Home by Choice* (Sisters, OR: Multnomah Publishers, 2000), 209.

3. Richard Swenson, *The Overload Syndrome* (Colorado Springs: NavPress, 1998), 65.

4. Anne Morrow Lindbergh, *Gift From the Sea* (New York: Pantheon Books, 2005 edition), 107.

5. Jacoba Urist, quoting Brigid Schulte, in "'Overwhelmed' Moms Choose Not to Be Busy," *The Today Show*, April 13, 2014, www.today.com/parents/overwhelmed-moms-choose-not-be-busy-2D79513957.

Cheri Fuller is a gifted speaker and award-winning author of more than forty-five books, including *What a Son Needs From His Mom* and the bestselling *When Mothers Pray, Raising Motivated Kids*, and *A Busy Woman's Guide to Prayer*. Her books have been translated into many languages.

As a popular speaker at conferences and retreats, Cheri has provided encouragement to people throughout the United States and other countries. A former Oklahoma Mother of the Year, Cheri has been a frequent guest on national TV and radio programs. Her articles on family, spiritual growth, relationships, and prayer have appeared in *Family Circle, Focus on the Family, Guideposts,* and many other publications.

Cheri holds a master's degree in English literature and is executive director of the nonprofit organization Oklahoma Messages Project. She and her husband, Holmes, have three grown children and six wonderful grandchildren.

Cheri's books, Bible studies, and other resources can be found at www.cherifuller.com, along with information on her speaking topics and how to schedule Cheri for events. You can contact her at cheri@cherifuller.com.

More From Cheri Fuller

If you've ever felt like your son is from a different planet, don't worry! There's a good reason why he perplexes you. Boys really do think, communicate, and process the world differently than girls. But no matter your son's age, he needs you.

Drawing from her own experiences and those of other moms and sons, Cheri Fuller shares what makes boys tick and how to become a more welcome influence at every stage in their lives. She answers all the top questions, including:

- "How can I help my son (and me!) deal with his emotions in a healthy way?"
- "My son hardly says a thing. What can I do?"
- "What are the best ways to instill good values?"
- "How can I encourage a lasting faith in God?"

With page after page of use-it-today advice and encouraging stories, this book will help you steer your son toward becoming a caring, confident young man.

What a Son Needs From His Mom

BETHANYHOUSE